The Cann

Cannabis Business Book

How to Succeed in Weed According to 50 Industry Insiders

Michael Zaytsev

Michael Zaytsev

.

ISBN-13: 9781724671554

Dedication

I dedicate this book to my parents and grandparents who are the greatest models of dedication I have ever known.

Thank you for birthing, raising, and loving me.

On 4/20/1991, with no assets and no English language skills, my entire family immigrated to America. I was about 17 months old and my big brother was almost 5 years old.

Together, through immense dedication, hard work, tenacity, and a whole lot of love, my parents and grandparents succeeded in providing me and my brother with a safe, happy, and beautiful childhood.

Their strength, sacrifices, and leadership afforded me the opportunity to live the American dream and to become who I am today.

This book is as much a part of their legacy as it is mine.

I consider my immigrant parents and grandparents to be the ultimate entrepreneurs. Against all odds, they turned nothing into something.

I love you. Thank you.

In loving memory of Arthur Dudin.
I get high on your memory.

All Praise To The Most High

Michael Zaytsev

Your Bonus Videos:

<u>Exclusive interviews</u> with 35+ of the Cannabis industry insiders featured in this book!

Over 15 hours of *never before seen* footage!

Available for you now at:
<u>www.MichaelZaytsev.com/bookbonus</u>

TABLE OF CONTENTS

Part I:
Planting Seeds

"CANNABIS
IS THE
FASTEST-GROWING
INDUSTRY
IN AMERICA,
AND
IT'S SOMETHING
THAT'S SAVING
A LOT OF
LIVES."

1.
Let's Get High

Congratulations! If you're reading this, you've chosen to make a wise, high-yielding investment in yourself and your Cannabis business career.

You're likely a mover, a shaker, a hustler, risk taker, rule breaker, lawmaker, a banker, a wanker, a gangster, a schemer, a dreamer, or maybe even a nonbeliever.

Whatever your background, you are about to discover:

* why Cannabis business represents an unprecedented once-in-a-lifetime opportunity for wealth creation and social impact
* how to take advantage of that opportunity
* whether or not the Cannabis business is right for you (it's not for everyone…)
* how the Cannabis industry differs from every other industry in the world
* the language of Cannabis industry insiders and what not to say in front of them if you want to be taken seriously
* the mindset, leadership principles, and best practices of highly successful Cannabis entrepreneurs
* how to raise money for your Cannabis business
* how to build a potent and supportive Cannabis network
* the most common mistakes Cannabis entrepreneurs make and how to avoid them
* what the highest yielding, lowest risk Cannabis

investment you can make today is

* how a successful Cannabis business can completely transform your life, create generational wealth, and have global impact across humanity

...and much more.

This book is designed to deliver a massive dose of value to whomever is bold, daring, and caring enough to read it.

But reading it is not enough!

You must also be willing to put the wisdom I've cultivated, processed, packaged, and delivered to you in your proverbial pipe and smoke it! Let it take you higher by taking <u>courageous, intentional action</u>.

> "I get by with a little help from my friends. I get high with a little help from my friends."
>
> —The Beatles

I have spent the last 6 years learning from the founding mothers and fathers of the American legal Cannabis industry and have personally been involved in shaping the philosophical, political, economic, and cultural landscape of this industry. Before I discovered my passion for Cannabis education, I worked in Silicon Valley, at Google, and in high finance, at J.P. Morgan.

As an author and Cannabis community organizer, I have personally educated thousands of people about the virtues of Cannabis.

As a Cannabis connector, I've facilitated countless Cannabis business connections and have co-produced over a million Cannabis-positive media impressions.

As a Cannabis business coach, I've helped my clients become the highest versions of themselves, while growing mission-driven businesses that make the world a better place.

This book will help you to do the same.

Here's the bad news: you're going to do all the hard work, because I can't do it for you. You must be willing to go beyond your comfort zone, take smart risks, and put in the hours. Unfortunately, you won't succeed in weed by sitting on the couch ripping the bong. Fortune favors the bold, and the bold take action.

On that note, I congratulate you for taking the action of purchasing this book.

What you'll find in this book is the wisdom I've gathered by interviewing (and working with) 50 of the Cannabis industry's most successful and prominent leaders, many of whom are the pioneers of legal Cannabis business.

Yes, it's great to have friends in high places!

What is it that all the highest achievers in Cannabis business have in common?

What allows them to succeed and stand out in an incredibly competitive business environment?

I'll tell you: we approach Cannabis business, and Life itself, with higher sensitivity, higher standards, and higher consciousness.

This book is infused with those elements of a higher mindset. While reading this book, you will learn how to develop the higher mindset that is indispensable for success in the Cannabis industry.

Spoiler alert: success in this industry is defined by putting ethics and higher standards at the forefront of everything you do. If that doesn't sound like you, you can stop reading now.

Or keep reading if you want to discover the exact strategies and tactics that transformed me from an idealistic 24-year-old stoner with absolutely no knowledge of Cannabis—except how to consume it—into one of the Cannabis industry's most consistently innovative, influential, and effective leaders.

Believe me: if I can do it, you can do it too.

Let's roll.

2.
Hi Mike Z

"You're the luckiest guy in the world."

That's what the doctor told me after I woke up from emergency surgery after a freak accident nearly took my life.

One very unremarkable Sunday afternoon, my 23-year-old self went to open the living room window in my San Francisco apartment. I was feeling pretty lucky: I was healthy, happily employed at Google, and was about to enjoy some of the Bay Area's finest Girl Scout Cookies —and not the kind that you eat.[1]

I wanted to be a considerate roommate, so I decided not to hot box the apartment and went to open the window. I soon discovered, in the worst way, that no good deed goes unpunished.

The large, old window shattered when I tried to slide it open.

Several shards of glass sliced into my arms giving me multiple wounds, including a gash several inches wide and bone deep.

I saw a chunk of meaty flesh hanging out of my right forearm.

Blood was fountaining out of my arm across the room.

Needless to say, I did not get around to enjoying Girl Scout

---

[1] This was back in 2013, when GSC was still relatively exotic Cannabis varietal, before Wedding Cake, Gelato, Runtz, and other offshoots were available.

Cookies that Sunday afternoon.

My buddy who witnessed this horrorshow called 911. Within minutes, paramedics were on the scene bandaging my arm and escorting me into an ambulance.

I was in excruciating pain and I couldn't feel nor move two of the fingers on my right hand—and, yes, I'm right handed.

In the Emergency Room, I learned that's what happens when your muscles, nerve, and tendons get severed completely.

At this point, I began seriously questioning my luck.

A few hours later, I awoke from surgery, and Dr. Safa[2] told me I was the luckiest guy in the world.

Was I on morphine, or was he the one tripping?

He explained that I had a Martin-Gruber Anastomosis in my right arm, something only 10 - 20% of people have. It meant that my ulnar nerve, which got sliced through completely by the glass, and my median nerve have a bridge connecting them. As a result, there was a good chance my right hand and fingers would not be completely paralyzed.

I was feeling a little less unlucky, but definitely nowhere near "luckiest guy in the world" status.

Dr. Safa went on to explain that normally, the ulnar nerve runs side by side, in tandem, with the ulnar artery. Had I been more "normal," my ulnar artery would have gotten sliced through and,

---

[2]Thank you Dr. Safa, you're the man!

in about 5 minutes or less, I'd have bled out and died.

My ulnar artery, however, was several inches away from where it is "supposed to be" in my arm.

After this anatomy lesson from my surgeon, I became overcome with emotion and burst into tears.

Sometimes, not being like everyone else can literally save your life. My difference saved mine, in more ways than one.

Crying in my hospital bed, I felt extremely lucky to be alive and deeply grateful to have excellent medical insurance through Google.

Then and there, I promised myself that I would try my best to never take my health and my Life for granted.

But still, I didn't exactly feel like the luckiest guy in the world.

Today, I look back at my traumatic accident and consider it to be one of the best things that's ever happened to me.

Without it, I'd probably still be an employee at Google, still living in the Bay Area, and maybe I'd know some cool people who were entrepreneurs in the Cannabis industry, but I doubt I'd be one. I'm pretty sure that if it weren't for my accident, I'd never have had all the amazing Cannabis business adventures I've been blessed with and I definitely would not have written two books before age 30.

After surgery, I went on disability leave and moved back home to New York City to be under my family's care. For several months,

I was bedridden as my arm healed from surgery.

In just a few weeks, I had gone from a thriving 23-year-old yuppie, to a disabled, dependent 24-year-old who had to learn how to brush his teeth and wipe his arse with his left hand.

My right arm, which had to be immobilized to protect the surgical repairs, began to form some seriously stubborn scar tissue in the elbow joint.

It took me literally hundreds of hours of painful physical therapy over the next five years to recover function and mobility in my right arm and hand. It was during this process that I discovered the power of Cannabis for pain management. I had previously been a "recreational" user,[3] now I'd understood what it meant to need Cannabis as medicine, for healing and pain relief.

Beyond that, I began meditating to help deal with the pain of physical therapy. Now, I'm a big advocate for mindfulness practice and am proud that I've helped 100% of my non-meditating coaching clients cultivate and sustain a meditation habit. If you don't already meditate, I highly recommend you start ASAP, the benefits are vast and undeniable.

When I became healthy enough to return to work, I took a job selling software at a hot, enterprise tech startup called BetterCloud (which would be a great name for a weed company). After 6 months of working there, I found myself miserable.

---

[3]This is a term many industry leaders do not like. It demeans the plant and makes light of its therapeutic power. Even though some people use Cannabis for fun, the term recreational is simply not accurate for most non-medical use cases. I only use it here to facilitate this teaching moment because I love you.

Although I was doing well at work and the company was growing, I felt completely unfulfilled. Selling software to businesses to help them manage their employees felt void of any sense of higher purpose.

While recovering from my near death accident and traumatic injuries, I began to explore questions of spirituality for the first time in my young life.

Why did this "freak" accident happen to me? How come I made it out alive? Was the force of bad "luck" that broke the glass the same force of good "luck" that spared my Life? Was there a greater purpose for my Life? What was I put on this Earth to do? Why was I alive?

Although I didn't have any good answers to these questions, it became abundantly clear to me that Life was not to be taken for granted, for it can be taken from you at any moment—and it only takes a moment.

I decided I couldn't afford to waste the prime years[4] of my life being bored, working at a job that didn't inspire me, or feeling like I wasn't contributing to the world around me.

So I quit my job to pursue my dream. Since middle school, before I even knew what it meant, I imagined growing up to be a businessman. After reading *The 4-Hour Work Week* in college, I knew I wanted to be my own boss, chart my own course, and make a real difference in the world.

---

[4]Whatever years you're in right now are your prime years. The past is gone and the future isn't guaranteed. There's only right now.

Through deep introspection, I crafted a vision for the lifestyle I wanted—a digital nomad lifestyle—and began strategizing to figure out what kind of business I could succeed in with my existing skills.

I considered Malcolm Gladwell's 10,000-hour rule from his best-selling book *Outliers*, which posits that it takes 10,000 hours of diligent, high-quality practice to achieve mastery in any discipline.

What did I want to master?

I knew it wasn't selling enterprise software.

Higher Mike Z

Since my halcyon days at Stuyvesant High School, where I picked up my first ever self-help book, *How to Win Friends and Influence People*, I'd been a personal development junkie.[5] Together with my communication skills and desire to help people, I realized I could succeed financially and enjoy personal fulfillment as a life coach, helping others achieve greater purpose, power, and prosperity in their lives.

Teaching something is the best way to learn it, and by teaching personal leadership skills and high performance habits to others, I'd give myself a chance at mastering those disciplines for myself. I figured if I could get 10,000 hours of experience being a great

---

[5]It was also at Stuy High where I discovered two of my Life's greatest passions, besides personal development: Cannabis and community leadership (through my service in student government as Sophomore Class President and CFO).

human being[6] before my mid thirties, then I'd set myself up for long-term success in both my professional life and personal life.

So I got trained and certified in Life Coaching, hired a business coach, worked diligently on developing myself, and changed my own habits and lifestyle.

I've been hustling and working on my own personal development ever since. And along the way, I started living my dream Life of being an entrepreneur.

Within a year, I was making more money as an entrepreneur across 3 business ventures than I did as a full time employee at BetterCloud, while working less than half the hours.[7]

My luck had changed.

With all the newfound free time, I began attending more and more events. One day, an old school chum of mine invited me to check out a Cannabis meetup. The rest, as they say, is history.

There, I discovered what I believed to be the reason I was put on this Earth, the reason for my traumatic freak accident, and the reason I had survived it.

At the meetup I met Dana Beal, an OG[8] and revolutionary

---

[6]Loving, loved, happy, healthy, independent, compassionate, intelligent, and well-rounded were some of the ways I defined that.

[7]To be clear, at the start of my entrepreneurial journey, I was working anywhere from 10 - 16 hours a day, 7 days a week. I loved it and it didn't feel like work. After a year, I got to a place where I could work 5 - 15 hours a week and still earn more than an adequate living.

[8]OG = Original Gangster or Original Gangsta, depending on who you ask

Cannabis activist who has been fighting for Cannabis freedom for over 50 years now! He organized smoke-ins on the White House lawn, founded the global marijuana march, and had been to prison multiple times for supplying pounds of pot to medical patients before dispensaries were a thing. He shared old activist war stories that amazed me and completely blew my mind.

I also met a young lady who suffered a traumatic brain injury from a motorcycle accident and who relied on Cannabis concentrates (something I'd never even heard of back in 2014) to keep her brain from swelling. She taught me about dabbing and also opened my eyes to the fact that Cannabis medicine was a real thing, not just a punchline to a cheesy glaucoma joke. Her story made me feel ashamed of all the times I'd previously made those thoughtless jokes.

I spoke with a guy my own age, an immigrant who grew up in Brooklyn just like me, discovered Cannabis in high school just like me, and needed financial aid to pay for college just like me.

Unlike me, however, he was a man of color. After a stop-and-frisk, which was routine in his neighborhood and unthinkable in mine, he was arrested for "marihuana"[9] possession. Because of that arrest, he became ineligible for financial aid and as a result could not afford to go to college.

He was an honors student and would have been the first person in his family to go to college. Instead, he now struggled to find employment and help his immigrant parents deal with the high cost of living in NYC.

---

[9]"Marihuana" is how it appears in the New York State Penal Code § 221.05

His story left me heartbroken. Why was this upstanding, young man robbed of the American dream because of a little Cannabis in his pocket?

That evening revealed to me that despite being a blissful Cannabis consumer for many years, I didn't know anything about the plant that had played such an important role in my life.

Cannabis was the glue that bonded many of my closest friendships, yet I had been living under a cloud of privileged ignorance when it came to Cannabis and had never even thought to learn anything about its history.

How come none of my 420-friendly friends (or weed dealers) had ever told me about the ugly, racist history of Cannabis prohibition?[10]

How come nobody ever told me the "War on Drugs" was really a war on people of color?

How come nobody ever told me about the versatility of hemp and how America was built on it?

I was furious.

After my outrage subsided, I realized that most people—even those who loved Cannabis like I did—were ignorant about the plant.

That night, I decided that for the rest of my life, I'd work in

---

[10] *13th* is a phenomenal documentary which lays out the deeply problematic realities of mass incarceration in America. It's a must watch if you intend to work in this industry and, more importantly, if you want to undo racism in America.

service of the Cannabis plant. I could no longer be a free rider, one who derived value from the plant but did not give anything back to the plant.

I refused to be a user. I would no longer stand idle as the plant was used as an instrument of oppression.

The coach in me decided the best way for me to educate myself was to start educating other people about Cannabis. I knew the best way to become a Cannabis leader was to create other Cannabis leaders, and so began my service to High NY, producing Cannabis community education opportunities and networking events in New York City.

Life has demonstrated to me time and time again the power of the Cannabis plant to uplift, heal, and inspire people.

What if humanity harnessed and utilized all of the plant's powers for healing and growth?

What would the world look like if people everywhere respected, cherished, nurtured, and worked in harmony with Mother Nature?

I knew if I dedicated my life to helping create that world, I'd die with no regrets about how I spent my time.

My mission became to make sure that as many humans as possible get as much benefit from Cannabis as possible.

My family immigrated to America from the former Soviet Union as asylum-seeking refugees when I was a baby. We arrived in New York City on April 20, 1991. Fighting for Cannabis freedom is my destiny. That's what I was born to do. That's what I will be doing until the day I die.

The fight is far from over, and I hope that by the time you finish this book, you'll be ready to join me in the fight for Cannabis freedom.

Judging by the results of the past six years (more on that soon), it seems like I made the right decision.

Now, I have no doubt about it and I'm constantly reminded of it: I am the luckiest guy in the world.

Every day, I make money doing something that I love: I educate those who are not connected to Cannabis so they can understand the far-reaching benefits the plant can offer humanity and how we can leverage its power to heal people and the environment while creating inclusive and regenerative economies.

Every day, I make money doing something that I love: I help caring and compassionate people who are discouraged or unclear to discover their highest purpose and the higher power within so they can live more authentic, inspired and fulfilling lives.

Every day, I make money doing something that I love: I help highly motivated, mission driven entrepreneurs grow profitable Cannabis businesses that uplift communities and make the world a better place.

If you suspect your calling might be in Cannabis, please don't wait for a near-death experience[11] to answer the call. Do it now.

---

[11]Everyone has trauma in their lives. Often, that trauma is forced upon us,

It's time.

As you read this book, allow me (with a little help from my friends) to be your Cannabis Business Coach, so that you, too, can feel like the luckiest person in the world, making money every day doing something that you love while also making a positive difference in this world.

---

beyond our control. How we respond, however, is within our control. Traumatic stress is a given, but post traumatic growth is a choice you must make. One of the best books on the subject of trauma, how it works, and how to heal it is _The Body Keeps the Score_.

3.

The High R.O.I. Promise

My promise is to give you 10,000% return on your financial investment with this book.

That's pretty high ROI[12] if you ask me. That means for your $20 purchase you're getting at least $2,000 worth of value in this book.

On top of that, I believe you'll also gain knowledge and insights from this book that will save you many hours of research, mistakes, frustration—or worse, inaction.

You might be thinking to yourself, *"Mike Z, how the hell are you going to give me $2,000 worth of value with this book?"*

Thanks for asking.

What would you pay to have an intimate conversation with the founder and owner of California's largest medical dispensary, a man with decades of Cannabis business experience?

What about the investors funding the biggest deals in Cannabis?

Or the Chief Mentor for the largest network of high-net-worth Cannabis investors in the world?

Maybe you'd prefer to chat with the attorneys who helped change and write the laws that legalized Cannabis in California,

---

[12]Return On Investment

Colorado, Florida, and Massachusetts?

How much do you think the people above charge for an hour of their time?

If you tried to connect with all of the people above and dozens more like them, do you think you'd have to spend more than $2,000? How many hours do you think it'd take for you to identify and meet all those people?

Here's the good news, you can have an intimate conversation with all of the people above and more as my gift to you.

Head over to MichaelZaytsev.com/bookbonus and you can get access to all those intimate conversations for free right now. Told you you were going to be doing all the hard work.

Do you think you'd get $2,000 of value asking those people for advice about Cannabis business? Do you believe speaking with them would be time well spent that may save you several hours of misguided, ineffective work? If yes, then I've made good on my promise and you haven't even read the book yet.[13]

If not, then allow me to share a little about my work so you feel confident that I'm qualified to serve as your Cannabis Business Coach.

If you're already convinced, feel free to skip the next section and jump into Chapter 5. Otherwise, keep reading to do your due diligence on my Cannabis credentials and contributions.

---

[13]Want to create raving fans? Always over deliver value to your customers. Give them more than they expect from you.

4.

Mike Z's Street Cred

Since 2014, I've poured my heart and soul into serving the Cannabis community and into helping Cannabis entrepreneurs succeed. In my humble (and biased) opinion, I've yielded remarkable results. I invite you to judge for yourself.

As the Founder of High NY, I have built and continue to lead one of the world's largest IRL[14] communities of Cannabis activists and entrepreneurs.

Along the way, I've produced dozens of Cannabis events that have educated and inspired thousands of New Yorkers. I have also co-created content that has reached over a million people, spreading responsible, Cannabis-positive messaging while challenging anti-Cannabis stigmas.

I've coached dozens of entrepreneurs, advocated for patients, lobbied politicians, and have empowered passionate citizens to become engaged, effective activists.

I've produced groundbreaking events including the New York City Cannabis Film Festival (NYC's first), the High Tech Hackathon (California's first ever Cannabis-focused hackathon), and the Cannabis Media Lab (the world's first media-focused business accelerator for Cannabis entrepreneurs).

I've hosted a fundraiser for longtime Cannabis champion,

---

[14]IRL = in real life. Good old fashioned, face-to-face human interaction.

Oregon Congressman, Earl Blumenauer, founder of the Congressional Cannabis Caucus and leader of the House Ways and Means Trade Subcommittee. My efforts helped him raise thousands of dollars for his Cannabis Fund—a political action committee geared toward ousting prohibitionist lawmakers.

I also had the high honor of personally introducing him to New York State Assemblyman Richard Gottfried, who like Congressman Blumenauer has been fighting for sensible Cannabis policy for decades, and who has done more advocacy for Cannabis issues than any other elected official in New York.

In 2017, I was honored for my work with a Cannabis Business Award.

I've had the pleasure of being a judge for multiple *High Times* Cannabis Cups in numerous categories.[15]

As a Cannabis thought leader, I've been invited to speak on CBS News, TEDx, Cheddar, Vulture, at over a dozen conferences around the country, and on several podcasts. My opinions have been solicited and quoted in the media in publications like *The Guardian, The New York Post, Complex, Village Voice, Mic, Inc., Vice, Timeout New York, Crain's,* and *Mashable.* And I never spent a penny on PR; they came to me.

As a writer, my insights on Cannabis business topics have appeared on Forbes.com, Entrepreneur.com, International Business Times, MindBodyGreen.com, Herb.com, and in Entrepreneur magazine.

---

[15]It's a tough job, but somebody's gotta do it. ;)

My first book, *The Entrepreneur's Guide to Cannabis*, appears on Ganjapreneur's and Women of Cannbiz's lists of best Cannabis books, has been a best seller on Amazon.com, and purchased by thousands of Cannabis entrepreneurs all over the world.

In Spring of 2019, the National Science Foundation invited me to work as a Cannabis industry mentor for scientists and PhD's in their Innovation Corps entrepreneurship training program.

Although I am extremely proud of my professional accomplishments, I share all the above not to show off, but rather to let you know two things. First, that you're in good hands. Second, that one person can have tremendous impact in this budding industry. I hope in sharing my story, I can embolden you to appreciate how powerful, productive, and impactful one individual—you—can be.

This book is the result of 6 years of my immersion and hard work in the Cannabis world. Because I did it, you don't have to reinvent the bong.

Please take the wisdom from this book and put it into productive action that supports the global Cannabis movement.

Together, in service to the Cannabis plant and a higher good, we can build a healthier, more prosperous future for humanity and for Mother Nature.

5.

The Cannabis Opportunity

According to the United Nations World Drug Report, global Cannabis demand is approximately $150 billion dollars a year. As of the writing of this book, the majority of that money still changes hands in the illicit, underground economy. It will still take several years for the remainder of that commerce to become legalized, taxed, and regulated.[16]

The re-legalization[17] of Cannabis is the biggest opportunity for entrepreneurs since the birth of the Internet—*if not bigger!*

Often, I am asked whether or not it is too late to enter the industry. When I wrote my first book, *The Entrepreneur's Guide to Cannabis* in 2016, the answer was absolutely not!

Now, even though the industry has matured, we're still only in the 2nd or 3rd inning of this ballgame. Cannabis industry dynamics have evolved significantly since 2016, and I expect we'll witness historic shifts over the next 5 - 10 years; the end of global Cannabis prohibition has never been closer.

---

[16]It's debatable whether or not governments should have the right to tax and regulate the Cannabis plant. This is especially hotly debated by OGs, purists, and those in legal states that do not allow home-grow or personal cultivation of Cannabis. Yes, it can be argued that if you need a license to buy, sell, or grow Cannabis, it isn't really free/legal. However, in this book I will not get into that highly charged, philosophical debate. For better or worse, all signs point to a future in which governments tax and regulate Cannabis commerce like they do with other agricultural commodities and medicines.

[17]After all, Cannabis used to be legal.

Is it too late to open a restaurant? Or start a clothing brand? No.

Cannabis has been around for a long time and it isn't likely to disappear anytime soon. There will always be a demand for it. Thus, it will never be too late to enter the Cannabis business. However, the industry is becoming more competitive and complex by the second.

One of the interview questions I asked everyone was, "What excites you most about the Cannabis business right now?"[18] Some answers below:

> "I think we're at the beginning of a huge, world-changing industry. It's not only the United States, it's all over the entire world. In 10 years, we'll look back and say what were people thinking [in keeping Cannabis illegal]?"
>
> —Alain Bankier,
> Founding Partner, New York Angels
> Executive Chairman, Nexien BioPharma, Inc.

> "The scale we're achieving right now. My ambition is that Cannabis makes its way into the medicine cabinet of every single family, everywhere around the world. We need a lot of people. We need a lot of companies. We need a lot of capital. We need a lot of legal changes to make that happen. What's most exciting to me is seeing the pace of that reform accelerate."
>
> —Steve DeAngelo,
> Co-Founder, Harborside Dispensary Group,
> The ArcView Group, & FLRish, Inc.,
> Author of *The Cannabis Manifesto*

---

[18]Interviews were conducted in 2017, 2018, and 2019.

THIS IS THE FASTEST-GROWING INDUSTRY IN AMERICA, YET IT'S SOMETHING THAT'S SAVING A LOT OF LIVES

"How many lives we can save [with Cannabis]? You see so many industries that really aren't good for people that are just growing, but not at this exponential rate. This is the fastest growing industry in America, yet it's something that's saving a lot of lives and creating huge revenues for the state."

—Chloe Villano,
President & Founder, Clover Leaf University

"The incredible medical potential of this plant. It was part of the traditional human diet, especially because most livestock animals consumed it. Cannabinoids have been part of the human diet for as long as we've been humans. One of the things that we're seeing is that there's a lot of diseases that can be alleviated, helped, or cured with Cannabinoid intake. This is one of the most important and powerful things about this plant moving out of prohibition is that there's a huge, huge number of medical uses for it."

—Casey O'Neil,
Founder, HappyDay Farms
Mendocino Chair, California Growers' Association

"The shift from a cottage industry run by proverbial mom-and-pop ownership moving towards an institutional industry, run by experienced management teams, with real boards of directors, funded by the private equity and venture capital community."

—Scott Grieper,
President & Founder of Viridian Capital Advisors

"Seeing the elite professional and academic world becoming interested in Cannabis and to see what kind of research, partnerships, and advances in social justice will come out of that. The adoption is happening very quickly."

—Shanel Lindsay,
Founder & President, Ardent Cannabis
Member of the Massachusetts Cannabis Advisory Board

"I'm excited about the eventual decriminalization and de-scheduling of Cannabis. The MORE Act, which represents the first comprehensive Cannabis reform legislation, could make this a reality. Whether it's the passing of the MORE Act by the House or another political act, Cannabis legalization is going to happen."

—Laura Lagano, MS, RDN, CDN
Co-Founder, Holistic Cannabis Academy

"Outside of marijuana, we've got hemp. I think it's going to be a much larger industry than even medical or social use Cannabis…In 50 years, we'll see Cannabis and hemp involved in every aspect of our life."

—Kayvan Khalatbari,
Founding Partner, Denver Relief, Denver Relief Consulting,
Board of Directors, Minority Cannabis Business Association

"The fact that *we* get to make one, that's what excites me. In previous industries there was a buy-in to being able to make a living or make money in that industry, and that buy-in had a lot to do with your gender, your race, and your economic status. Unfortunately, we're seeing some of those same ideals seep into the Cannabis industry, especially as we start to see legalization move into other states. However, I think that more so than any other industry we have some wild thinkers, some people who have a lot of revolutionary ideas—not just about Cannabis, but about other social problems—that stand to make a lot of money in this industry, and I'm hopeful that will result in a shift of power where the people that are the free thinkers, the people that are caring about social justice issues will have a seat at the table with all of the people that got where they are because of their status."

—Amanda Reiman, PhD
Director of Community Relations, Flow Kana[19]

"The thing that I'm most excited about is that we're able to create a whole new industry from the ground up. All these rules that are being enacted, all this legislation that is going to be implemented is going to be done for the first time. When do you ever get that [as] an entrepreneur? So I'm excited to do it the right way and hopefully by the values that we've learned from a lot of people within the community to push it forward."

—David Hua,
Co-Founder & CEO, Meadow

"This is the time to get involved. We're still at the dawn of what is going to be an incredible industry and the

---

[19]My interview with Amanda took place well before Feb 2019 in which Flow Kana raised $125 million dollars. I bet she was pretty excited about that.

power to shape that industry is in the hands of entrepreneurs. The power to alter that future is in your hands, so get out there and do good business [by creating] a marijuana economy that stays true to the ideals of treating people right, eliminating social injustice and racial disparity."

—Brian Vicente,[20]
Founding Partner, Vicente Sederberg LLC

When it comes to Cannabis business, there's plenty to be excited about. I find myself thrilled by all of the above answers and I'm not even high right now! Take a moment to consider what about the Cannabis industry most excites you. Write it down.[21]

For me, it's that this industry provides the unique, hybrid possibility for simultaneously doing good and doing well at the highest levels. That means you can make a lot of money while also helping to address some of the worst mistakes of the previous generations.

The Intersectional Nature of Cannabis

No doubt, the opportunity to create generational wealth is what draws many people to Cannabis investment and entrepreneurship. Even cooler than that, Cannabis business has the potential to positively impact the lives of billions of people and therefore to dramatically alter the future of human

---

[20]Brian's firm, Vicente Sederberg, helped craft the law that legalized Cannabis in Colorado. In our interview, Brian shares a great story about how important it is to involve local communities in the campaigns that are being designed to reach and serve them.

[21]Once you finish the book, check if it's still the thing that most excites you.

civilization as we know it.

Now this may sound like flowery rhetoric, and I very much enjoy flowery rhetoric—especially pot puns—however, this is no exaggeration.

Cannabis already is, and will continue to be, a gateway to reforming several institutions—healthcare, government, criminal justice, agriculture, energy, etc.—many of which, in my judgement, are critically flawed, failing, and in desperate need of a revolution.

The most successful Cannabis entrepreneurs recognize that Cannabis business offers more than just the chance to transform their personal lives and finances.

WHAT MOTIVATES THE GREATEST LEADERS IN CANNABIS BUSINESS IS THE OPPORTUNITY TO POSITIVELY IMPACT HUMANITY'S FUTURE.

This isn't just the making of a new industry; it's a paradigm shift in global consciousness.

> "[This is] a once-in-a-civilization opportunity to redefine what we want for the future of agriculture."
>
> —Casey O'Neil,
> Founder, HappyDay Farms
> Mendocino Chair, California Growers' Association

I had the pleasure of interviewing Casey O'Neil multiple times and each conversation was an inspiring and illuminating experience. Casey is a modern day Renaissance man and philosopher king who shares my affinity for Borat jokes.

Seriously though, Casey's intellect is high-grade, top-shelf, and no-joke, which makes him a pleasure to chat with.

In addition to running his family farm, Casey also serves as a leader for his community. He advocates on behalf of California growers to preserve environmentally responsible policies, opportunities for small, independent farmers, and for Cannabis purity.

Be like Casey.

Once upon a time at the Emerald Cup, Casey kindly gifted me a jar of his delicious, organic, sun-grown flowers.

For the next few days, I walked around with that jar, opening it every few minutes, and taking a deep whiff of the flowers. The terpenes were so rich and the sweet strawberry fragrance so delicious, that I just couldn't stay away. The best thing about this aroma was that it literally smelled like clean, sustainable, and ethical Cannabis.

> "It's so dope because you can literally create your own world. I suffer from lupus disease, and that's kind of how I came up with *Leisure Life*; it's like I want to be able to chill and do what I want. So I created a brand around that, and that's really what the Cannabis industry is about right now: you can literally create the world that you want, which is amazing."
>
> —Amber Senter,
> CEO, Leisure Life Products
> Co-Founder & Executive Director, Supernova Women

The thing I love most about Cannabis business is that it has created a space for creative, driven people to empower themselves to define their own realities.

Cannabis business transformed my Life. I used to be chained to my desk. Now, I wake up whenever I want, work on whatever I want, and often feel like the luckiest guy in the world.

> "The sky's the limit. You can really write your own ticket as long as you do it in a collaborative manner, there is an opportunity for all of us today to win. Find your swim lane. Figure out what you want to do and what you're best at doing."
>
> —Giadha Aguirre De Carcer,
> Founder & CEO, New Frontier Data

The scale, ubiquity, and intersectional nature of Cannabis offers entrepreneurs, investors, and innovators the chance to transform their lives, change the world, and make lasting social impact.

The next section is all about how to make that happen.

Part II:
How to Succeed in Weed

"NO
AMOUNT OF
CAPITAL,
COMPETENCE,
OR CHARISMA
CAN MAKE
UP
FOR A
LACK OF
CHARACTER."

6.
The Most Important Cannabis Business Decisions

> "Watch your thoughts, they become your words; watch your words, they become your actions; watch your actions, they become your habits; watch your habits, they become your character; watch your character, it becomes your destiny."

—Lao Tzu,
Master of Going with the Flow

You live and die based on your mindset. It's the single most important factor that will determine the quality of your Life and the success of your business.

It's not uncommon to hear stories of rich and famous people who seem to have it all yet are so depressed and in so much pain that they commit suicide.

On the flip side, when I travelled through Vietnam, a so-called Third World nation, I met people who lived in shacks, with few material possessions and difficult professions as laborers, yet who were full of joy and enthusiasm. How can that be? The difference is in the mindset.

My goal with this book is to teach you the higher mindset that has enabled me and all the Cannabis entrepreneurs featured in this book to succeed.

A strong, healthy mind yields productive thoughts which create powerful actions that compound into habits and results. Your mindset is your operating system. It determines your destiny.

Start With Why[22]

> "Why are you doing what you're doing? There's a very simple equation to success and it all starts with why. Everybody always wants to talk about how you do things, but that's not what makes you a success. If you really want to be a sensation, if you want to enter this industry and have longevity you do that by developing your why. With me and Magical Butter, my why was I believe that Cannabis is a dietary essential and I wanted to prove the point that if people ingested Cannabinoids overall they would feel better and have a sense of well-being. We've proved that thesis now for the last six years. [Magical Butter] has been very successful because I had a strong why. Develop your why."
>
> —Garyn Angel
> CEO, Magical Butter

Garyn is one of the most colorful, exuberant, and effective Cannabis executives out there. I'll never forget my first time meeting him.

It was the Winter of 2016, and I had fled New York's harsh winter to enjoy the palm trees and warmth of Miami. It was a magical time; bong rips and Cuban espressos fueled my productivity as I wrote the rough draft of my first book. One of

---

[22]If you want some help with this, there's a famous book and TED talk by Simon Sinek called "Start With Why".

my mentors connected me with Garyn, who is based in Florida.

Garyn invited me to dinner at The Grill in the Bal Harbour St. Regis. I hadn't packed any formal clothing for my trip and upon entering the 5-star hotel's gorgeous lobby, I felt woefully underdressed. Forget business attire and even business casual, I was in beach bum chic.

I walked into the steakhouse and Garyn, together with one of his associates, greeted me with a big, welcoming smile. He assured me I was about to have one of the most delicious dining experiences in all of Florida.

Before the waiter even came by to offer drinks, Garyn pulled out some homemade gummies and offered them to the table. After asking him how strong they were, I graciously accepted a gummy or two.

After we exchanged introductions and pleasantries, Garyn got right down to business, asking me about my work, High NY, my plans for the future, etc. His playful warmth had shifted into a deep, intense, almost ferocious focus as he listened to my story. I didn't realize I'd be getting grilled at the same time as my steak was.

I was glad that the questions hit me before the edibles did.

After giving Garyn my honest answers to his questions, he looked me right in the eyes and said, "Mike you're not doing enough. You can do better and you need to be doing more. You're doing all this great stuff but you don't know why..." It felt like a punch in the gut, and even though I didn't know it at the time, it was exactly what I needed to hear.

Fortunately, the edibles hit, the steaks arrived, and, as Garyn promised, I enjoyed a super delicious meal. For the next few days, I couldn't get Garyn's words out of my head. On one hand, I was disappointed and felt discouraged. On the other hand, I was fired up to know that a successful Cannabis business leader I looked up to believed that I had more to give and offer.

Like any good coach, Garyn challenged me to step my game up. It came as no surprise to me when I later found out he regularly mentors younger Cannabis entrepreneurs like Matt Gray, CEO of Herb.co, and my dear friend Sarah Stenuf, Founder of Veteran's Ananda. Why does he do that? Because he knows that leaders create leaders and "together we win."[23] Thanks for all you do Garyn.

Defining Success

In Stephen Covey's classic book, *7 Habits of Highly Effective People*, Habit #2 is to "Begin with the end in mind."[24] And so, to begin, we must define success.

Every successful human that I know creates SMART goals: Goals that are Specific, Measurable, Achievable, Relevant, and Time bound. Every business sprouts from a favorable vision of the future or, simply put, a goal. Choosing an intention or end game is one of the first and most important decisions you must make for your business.

---

[23]This is one of Garyn's favorite slogans and principles.
[24]Habit #1 is Be Proactive, which you're doing by reading this book.

Be SMART about it. It's pretty hard to succeed if you don't know what success looks like for you.

Here are the four essential questions for you to put in your proverbial pipe to puff on and ponder:

1. Why do you want to be in the business of Cannabis?
2. What do you want to accomplish by being in the Cannabis business? (be specific)
3. What kind of business do you want to build? What's the exit? Or are you interested in building a multi-generational empire? The Seagram's of Cannabis? If passive income is the goal, how much do you need?
4. What does success look like for you?

See it, hear it, feel it, smell it, breathe into it. Give it energy and believe it is possible and that you are worthy of it if you want to manifest it.

If I could wave a magic wand made of hemp and give you the wildest vision of Cannabis business success right now, what would that look like?

- How would Life be different for you?
- What would change for you?
- What's in your way of getting that?
- What are you willing to change, sacrifice or give up to get to your ideal future?
- How must you evolve in order to achieve that vision of success?
- How much time can you afford to give your business before it generates a consistent financial return for you?

I highly encourage you to write down the answers to all of the above questions and to revisit these questions and your answers regularly (monthly or quarterly). There will be times along your journey where struggle or sacrifice are required. When you face those tough times, remind yourself of your purpose with great clarity and enthusiasm. This will help you to fight through the resistance and challenges that you will undoubtedly encounter on your Cannabis entrepreneur's journey.

When I started my first business, life coaching for stressed out high-tech and high-finance professionals, my definition of success was to work remotely, for less than 20 hours a week, generating at least $5,000 of monthly revenue without taking on any debt or employees. I wanted to spend my free time traveling, reading, meeting people, and enjoying really dank Cannabis. I knew it wouldn't happen overnight, and so I gave myself a deadline of 12 months to get to that point.[25] I created a timeline of milestones, and SMART key performance indicators (KPIs) that allowed me to measure my progress along the way.

For the 24-year-old version of Michael Zaytsev, the above scenario was my definition of business success. One major reason I knew I had succeeded was because I created a definition for success that was SMART: specific, measurable, achievable, relevant, and time bound. After a year of hard work and calculated risk taking, I was able to easily determine that I had, in

---

[25]I also made sure I prepared enough financial cushion and a strict budget to allow myself the time and space needed to commit to achieving my definition of success. Don't take the risk of starting a business if it will seriously jeopardize your safety, security, and health.

fact, achieved success.[26]

I Wasn't Always So SMART

When I entered the Cannabis business, my definitions of success were bigger and broader than the ambitions I had for my coaching business. I wanted to inspire and empower other people who were passionate about Cannabis. I wanted to build a New York brand that the Cannabis community trusted, respected, and admired. I wanted to produce financial freedom for myself and my family. I wanted to create a world where every single human being is free to benefit from the magic of Cannabis and Mother Nature's other gifts as well.

Although those lofty goals fueled my motivation, they weren't very SMART. And once motivation wavered—as it inevitably will—I found myself dazed and confused. I was overwhelmed with possibilities of how to spend my time and money, and had no clue where my efforts would be best rewarded and how to prioritize. This is because I failed to prepare and, in doing so, I prepared to fail.

My lack of SMART goals (and KPIs) left me moving in the right direction, but without a tangible destination. This caused me to make the second most common mistake Cannabis Entrepreneurs tend to make: I lacked focus and was easily distracted by the seemingly never-ending, interesting opportunities that came across my desk.

Therefore, instead of taking the direct path to my destination, I

---

[26]Once you achieve success, you encounter a whole new set of challenges and will likely be required to re-answer some of these powerful questions.

took many side-trips, detours, and ultimately wasted time, energy, and gas money along the way.[27] If I had a clear endpoint or SMART definition of success, it would have been much easier to make better decisions about how to allocate my time and money in a way that got me to Cannabis business success much faster. That being said, I still did ok, because I was always clear on my values and my why which served as my (moral) compass. And I was absolute in my commitment to keep on trucking while enjoying the journey, regardless of bumps in the road. Of course, it didn't hurt that I already had a successful coaching business to finance my cost of living.

The Most Important Business Decisions

The critical decisions required for entering the Cannabis business are: 1) choosing to do so, 2) knowing why you're doing so, and 3) defining what success looks like for you.

Once those are squared away, the real fun begins.

Every successful entrepreneur I know knows how to make important business decisions. A question I asked every single person interviewed for this book was, "What are the most important decisions you make as a leader?" Most of them responded by mentioning one of the two major forces that influence all business decisions, including goals, no matter what industry you're in.

The brilliant Shanel Lindsay expressed both:
"The biggest and most important decisions are where are we

---

[27]Although the journey was scenic and a fun adventure with lots of greenery along the way. No regrets here.

going to spend our time and money, what opportunities are we going to pursue. You can't do everything. There's not enough hours in the day."[28]

Time and money are for your business what oxygen and food are for your body. They are the essentials and must factor into every business decision you make.

Master the forces of time and money, and success will flow naturally.

---

[28]Shanel is an attorney, Founder & President, Ardent Cannabis, & Member of the Massachusetts Cannabis Advisory Board

If you want to try any Ardent products check them out on ArdentCannabis.com use the promo code HIMIKEZ to save $$$ when you purchase their signature decarboxylator.

7.
The 10 Characteristics of Highly Successful Cannabis Entrepreneurs

It takes a whole lot more than a clear why, SMART goals, and astute decision making to succeed in Cannabis business.

Being your own boss, creating a sustainable, profitable Cannabis business, recruiting and managing employees, adhering to dynamic regulations, crisis management, etc. are all difficult processes. As a Cannabis entrepreneur, you will have to do all of the above, and much more, often while facing time pressure and financial constraints.

Good luck maintaining work-life balance and remaining sane while juggling all of the above. You'll need it.

If you think it sounds challenging, I'd argue that it's even harder than it sounds in a Cannabis industry that is becoming more competitive and complex by the second.

If you believe in history and statistics, then it might upset you to learn that the expected outcome of starting a business—especially for first time entrepreneurs—is failure.

More than 80% of all new ventures are out of business within 5 years; more than 95% are out of business within 10 years.

Imagine working day and night for 2, 3, 4, maybe even 5 to 10 years, only to have to shut down shop and move on. Approaching scary, bad odds (and big challenges) like that on a daily basis with a level of "LET'S GO!!!" enthusiasm is the kind of determination, grit, and perhaps irrational confidence, required to become successful in Cannabis business.

What's One Characteristic a Cannabis Entrepreneur Absolutely Must Have in Order to Succeed?

That's what I asked every single person I interviewed for this book in order to figure out what separates the winners, the cream of the crop, from the losers who are weeded out. Across over 50 interviews, the following 10 qualities were consistently reiterated.

There was a clear #1 answer, and then there was everything else.

By the way, most people I interviewed agreed that in order to succeed, you're going to need ALL 10 of these characteristics.

1) Grit
(a.k.a. Resilience, Persistence, or Determination)

> "Grit: there are going to be more no's that they will hear in their lifetime than yes's, but it only takes one yes."
>
> —David Hess,
> President & Co-Founder, Tress Capital

> "Persistence. I can't tell you how many times I got told no for the National Cannabis Festival. I can't tell you how many times in year one people weren't quite sure that this person on the other end of the phone could deliver all the things she was talking about, but I think that along with my team we've been very diligent and very thorough and very persistent so we are always rebooting, reorganizing, and finding new ways to

approach issues so that we can turn that no into a yes."

—Caroline Phillips,
Founder, National Cannabis Festival

"Resiliency and staying the course. There's only a certain percentage that actually succeed…because they're willing to keep going, they keep coming back, they keep coming back, they keep coming back. So every time you exhale, you just keep coming back and trying to improve what you do."

—Eileen Konieczny, RN
Author, *Healing With CBD*

"Determination. You can never give up, because it changes so often…new agencies come in to regulate you, you lose your bank account, you know things can be really rough when you're a business owner in this industry, so I think determination is probably the best thing I could say, you know. Never give up."

—Chloe Villano,
President & Founder, Clover Leaf University

"Determination. You got to be driven. You have to be willing to put in the extra hours, the hard work, the time, the effort, the energy. Then, you got to be willing to accept some setbacks. They say, 'the master has failed more times than the beginner has even tried.'"

—Casey O'Neil,
Founder, HappyDay Farms
Mendocino Chair, California Growers' Association

2) Flexibility

The Cannabis industry is like a homemade edible cooked by an amateur using illicit ingredients: highly unpredictable. Legal Cannabis business has never been done before and it changes very, very quickly. Brace yourself. Expect and anticipate change. The unexpected is all that's guaranteed.

Here's what the experts have to say on this:

> "You've got to be very resilient, but you also have to be flexible, and you have to know how to ride the waves. If you can't be flexible in something that's constantly changing, you'll likely have a lot of problems."
>
> —Amber Senter,
> CEO, Leisure Life Products
> Co-Founder & Executive Director, Supernova Women

> "You have to know how to execute. You have to know how to get shit done...Intertwined with that, you need to have an intellectual and mental flexibility to execute your plan. There's shit that happens that you can't predict, whether it's regulatory, whether it's political, whether it's business wise. You need to know when to zig and when to zag. So that flexibility combined with the ability to make stuff happen."
>
> —Alain Bankier,
> Founding Partner, New York Angels
> Executive Chairman, Nexien BioPharma Inc.

> "The willingness to get it done, to work hard and be extremely flexible. There's a bit of a contradiction because, on one hand you have to be laser focused on your goal, but on the other hand you have to be flexible enough to pivot when the circumstances make that the best path forward."
>
> —Mara Gordon,

Founder, Aunt Zelda's

3) Passion

The only way your business will work out—in Cannabis or any industry—is if your energy and desire is singularly focused. If you want to do this, there should be nothing else you'd rather be doing. The pros agree:

> "Find something that keeps you up at night and makes you jump out of bed every morning. If you are passionate about what you do, you will have the motivation you need to make it through the long journey of entrepreneurship."
>
> —David Tran,
> Co-Founder, Farechild & DOPE Magazine

> "You gotta have a passion for the plant or a passion for the industry—or the people in the industry—because it's a really hard industry and your passion is what propels you through the shit."
>
> —Johnny B.,
> Inventor and CEO, NoGoo

> "You're going to encounter a lot of bumps in the road: a lot of challenges, a lot of problems. And the only thing that's going to keep you on that path of success is really having a desire and a passion for what you do. So I would caution people, at the very outset, to really challenge themselves and do some introspection and decide if Cannabis is really the right industry for them...In order to ride the waves of this industry, the ups and downs, you're really going to have to have a passion for what you

do."

—Shanel Lindsay,
Founder & President, Ardent Cannabis
Member of the Massachusetts Cannabis Advisory Board

4) Vision (Creativity)

I've been pitched lots of Cannabis start-up ideas, and 99% have been duds from first glance. I don't even need to see the pitch deck or go over the financials when I can tell that the entrepreneur lacks a unique vision. Lacking creativity or vision means either trying to copy something that is already out there, without even knowing it or, worse, repeating an idea that has already failed multiple times. Success requires seeing an opportunity to solve a meaningful problem in a valuable way that no one has noticed before.

> "Without vision, even the most focused passion is a battery without a device."
>
> —Ken Auletta
> Journalist, *The New Yorker*

> "You have to have vision and outside-the-box thinking. The solution is not going to be there in front of you....We're working on things that have never been done before, so you have to have vision and you have to be solution oriented. I noticed that entrepreneurs and people that I've seen not be successful [make] a lot of excuses. 'I couldn't do this and I couldn't do that.' Well, you've got to figure out a way to get it done. Or a different way to get it done...I would sum it up as being creative in your solutions and your way of thinking is the way that you're going to find success."

—Shanel Lindsay,
Founder & President, Ardent Cannabis
Member of the Massachusetts Cannabis Advisory Board

"Have a strong vision and leadership skills. You have to convince people that what you're doing—even if they disagree with you—is not only going to work out the way you say it is, but it's going to be better than what they think it's going to be. You lead with that—a lot of charisma, backed by evidence that you can achieve [it]... When I started my Massachusetts registered marijuana dispensary application, we marched into Berkshire County in Massachusetts and told them, this is the way it's going to be, it's going to be fantastic, you're going to love it, we're gonna build this brand new building, how can we make this suitable for the city? I think it takes that attitude, where you're kind of reaching into the future and pulling it towards the present, so that people can see what you see clearly. So rendering that vision in its clarity and in its detail for other people and then getting them to sing the same tune, those are two very, very critical skills in the Cannabis industry."

—Nial DeMena,
CEO & Founder, Manna Molecular

5) A Plan

"Start with an idea of the problem you want to solve or help people with on a mass scale. Create everything from the top down. Start with the vision, [define] your purpose, what you want to accomplish both for yourself and for the industry, and create everything from there."

—Mike Garganese,

Co-Founder, Lola Lola, Hilani, & Pluto

More on this when I discuss the most common Cannabis business mistakes in chapter 11.

6) Work Ethic (Effort)

> "Work your ass off. I mean work your absolute ass off. Don't quit. If it takes 20 hours a day, work 21 and don't complain that you're working 21 hours a day because at the end of the day, you're not throwing shingles on roofs, you're not building blocks out in the sun, you're doing something that you love because you are passionate and at the same time you're helping your customers."

—Garyn Angel
CEO, Magical Butter

7) Courage

There's a lot of uncertainty in this field. If you want to be a trailblazer and make a fortune in Cannabis business, you're going to have to face the unknown and welcome it with open arms.

> "Fearlessness. There's still a tremendous stigma. There's still businesses that won't work with you because of the connection to Cannabis."

—Danny Danko,
Senior Cultivation Editor, *High Times*

> "An unrealistic risk tolerance. To be comfortable in Cannabis [as] an entrepreneur, which is hard, requires creativity and lots of long hours...But in Cannabis we are unrealistic about our risk, because every day I'm doing something that's federally illegal that I can go to jail for.

I've known people that have had their mortgages pulled because the bankers found out they're in the Cannabis space...So, again, the risks of getting into this [industry]: you have to be willing to break the law and be persona non grata at your bank and not be able to get a mortgage. You have to have a pretty thick skin, and you have to really believe that the payoff is going to be there, because there's an unbelievable amount of risk that we take to do this entrepreneurial effort."

—Christian Hageseth,
Founder, Green Man Cannabis and ONE Cannabis Group
Author of *Big Weed*

8) Focus

Christian Hageseth, author of *Big Weed*, founder of Green Man Cannabis and ONE Cannabis Group told me the most important decisions he makes as a Cannabis business leader are, "The things that we don't do.[29] It's the decisions that I make about what we keep off our collective consciousness in the company. There's a lot of opportunities, there's a lot of shiny objects out there, Cannabis is a very broad industry...You have to stay focused, you have to know what your one thing[30] is and stick to that."

"Discipline with a little fearlessness. Stay focused, execute one step at a time, don't try to do 50 things at once, do one thing better than everybody else."

—Asher Troppe,
CEO & Co-Founder, Tress Capital

---

[29] *Big Weed* I especially love this book's title because Christian Hageseth is a big dude. He looks like he could have been a linebacker for the Broncos.

[30] *The One Thing* & *Deep Work* - great books about building the skill of focus.

9) Integrity

Integrity is a non-negotiable requirement for success in Life. Regardless of the arena, those who truly earn greatness in their discipline are people of great integrity.

When I asked each of the Cannabis business leaders what qualities in potential partners are unacceptable for them, lack of integrity was always at the top of the list.

> "Lack of integrity and values—that's *the* deal breaker."
>
> —Christie Lunsford,
> CEO, The Hemp Biz Conference

10) Business Acumen

This one should be pretty obvious but in case it's not, you need business acumen to succeed in Cannabis business. It doesn't matter if you learned it on the streets, in schools, in corporate settings, or all of the above. At the end of the day, Cannabis business is a business. It's dollars and cents. Does your business make sense? Does it make dollars? Does it generate high ROI? Do you know how to build teams and manage people? Do you understand corporate governance? Do you understand that legal compliance is paramount or you can go to jail and lose everything? Can you sell and market a product or service? If not, you better learn. That being said, the Cannabis industry is a unique phenotype of business, which we will explore in the next chapter.

As you ponder how the 10 must-have characteristics of successful Cannabis entrepreneurs apply to you, consider this potent quote:

> "Tenacity, passion, tolerance of ambiguity—that is you don't always need to know exactly what's going on—a vision, a belief in self—that's self-confidence, not arrogance—some flexibility of course, and rule-breaking, you've got to be able to break the rules in order to move ahead. The one characteristic on top of all of that that's so important in my mind, that every entrepreneur in Cannabis must possess, is self-awareness. That is this: understanding their strengths and their flat spots."
>
> —Francis Priznar,
> SVP and Chief Mentor, The Arcview Group

8.

There's No Business Like Cannabis Business

"There is no Cannabis industry or market—there are [40+] separated markets and each one must be treated differently."

—Alain Bankier,
Founding Partner, New York Angels
Executive Chairman, Nexien BioPharma, Inc.

"Cannabis is a unique, fragmented and relatively inefficient market. In a lot of ways, I believe this provides real opportunity. An opportunity to mitigate these inefficiencies and tackle the unique needs that this industry has. As you look to develop products and services within the industry, really try to find a unique solution to a problem, whether that's an ancillary service like Headset that is tackling the data side of the industry or a new type of infused Cannabis product that is filling a consumer need."

—Cy Scott,
Co-Founder, Headset & Leafly

"You don't know what you're getting into. You need to have the love for what you're doing to succeed. I wouldn't recommend someone who's not into Cannabis to get into the Cannabis industry."

—Rhory Gould
CEO, Arborside Dispensary,
Winner of High Times Trailblazer award and 25+ Cannabis Cups

The creation of the legal Cannabis industry is the biggest opportunity for entrepreneurs since the birth of the internet. Cannabis business represents more than $150 Billion of annual demand.

Although the emerging Cannabis industry is often compared to the end of alcohol prohibition, that comparison is largely invalid. Alcohol was legal just a few years prior to the failed prohibition experiment. Cannabis is different. It hasn't been legal in almost a century. Besides, alcohol is truly a vice product, used primarily for intoxication. Cannabis is significantly more versatile.

In fact, Cannabis for medicinal use, Cannabis for personal use, and non-psychoactive Hemp for industrial use represent three entirely different industries that must be regulated separately. Many elected officials, policy makers, and Cannabis laypeople don't intuitively grasp why this is the only pragmatic approach. Some who are less informed want to treat the different varieties of the plant as one thing, with one set of rules to govern it. This kind of blanket approach is both irresponsible and irrational. When it comes to Cannabis utilization, intent matters.

It's Never Been Done Before

This has never been done before. There is no precedent for legitimizing and regulating the commercialization of Cannabis. Nobody knows exactly how it's going to unfold. Not one year from now, not five or ten years from now—certainly not fifty years from now.

It's an important and useful thought exercise for Cannabis

entrepreneurs to go through. Form an intelligent opinion on how the industry will look in the future and why. This will help to shape the vision for your Cannabis business and the trajectory of how it will evolve along with the industry.[31]

The legal Cannabis industry is already huge and it is rapidly expanding. Yet, there is still a great need for compassionate leaders who will shape the industry in a way that promotes restorative justice and compassion on a global scale.

> "Nobody has done this before; this is a new thing for every single person that's doing it, and whether you've built a thousand businesses in different industries or not, there's nothing really similar to this industry. I've spoken to really successful business people in other industries that have done multiple industries, and [Cannabis] is just unique…The one thing that I think is common among everyone is a lack of experience doing this exact thing."
>
> —Evan Nison,
> Founder & CEO, NisonCo PR
> Co-Founder, Whoopi & Maya

> "This is history in the making. This is something that's never happened before and will never happen again. We have a responsibility in that. So if folks are thinking that this is just something fun that they want to do: wait. Wait until the future of Cannabis legalization is not being held so delicately. We still have folks that are imprisoned for long periods of time for very minor Cannabis offenses. So until you're ready to engage in that work [of freeing them], be a fan, be a consumer, but don't be an industry

---

[31]I share my predictions for the future of Cannabis business in Chapter 17

person. Because we need to ensure that everybody has freedom from criminal prosecution for Cannabis before we can really start the party."

—Amanda Reiman, PhD
Director of Community Relations, Flow Kana

"There really is no precedent for this in American history. The movements for gay rights, civil rights, and women's rights all had major economic consequences for the country, but they didn't result in the emergence of brand new industries. The closest thing was the repeal of alcohol prohibition in 1933, but even that just re-legalized an industry that existed just a few years before. The marijuana industry really is unique."

—Ethan Nadelmann,
Founder, Drug Policy Alliance

11 Ways the Cannabis Industry is Unlike Any Other:

1) An agricultural commodity with multi-billion dollar, global demand is considered federally illegal in the U.S., yet there are 35 U.S. states where medical Cannabis is legal and in 15 states (plus Washington D.C.) adult use of Cannabis is legal too. Each state's legal market has completely different rules and regulations. Adult use of Cannabis is legal in Canada. More than 30 countries have legalized some form of Cannabis and are even engaging in legal international Cannabis trade.

2) There is direct competition with a well established, illicit, underground market.

3) Consumers are vastly under-informed, overly-forgiving, and used to acquiring products illegally, without much regard for quality control or safety standards. There is minimal

transparency into product quality and almost no accountability for producers and distributors in terms of consumer protection. This is especially true of the illicit market.[32]

4) Decades of anti-Cannabis propaganda must be undone. There is still a very real stigma against Cannabis and the people who consume, produce, and distribute it. Imagine if you grew up being told that drinking coffee would ruin your life and the people who use it are somehow worse than those who don't. This bias is institutionalized and plays out not only culturally, but also very practically as business service providers will think twice about working with you and often will treat you like a second-class citizen (or worse, a criminal) for being a Cannabis entrepreneur. On top of that, you will likely encounter anti-Cannabis prejudice in personal relationships from people who you thought were your friends.

5) As of June 1st 2020, Cannabis business operators, owners, and investors are still not able to reliably access banking resources. Billions of dollars of Cannabis transactions—paying taxes, salaries, vendors, etc.—continue to happen in cash. This is dangerous for so many reasons. Unfortunately, it's unsurprisingly common to hear about

---

[32]Don't say "the black market." Given the racial disparities in Cannabis policing and all the damage done to black communities, this has become a problematic term. By saying it you run the risk of offending Cannabis activists and advocates, especially those with melanin. Be sensitive to cultural differences.

Cannabis dispensaries, growers, or transporters being targeted by armed robbers.[33]

6) Section 280E of the federal tax code severely limits the expenses that businesses which produce, process, or sell Cannabis are able to write off. This creates an environment in which plant-touching Cannabis businesses pay an effective tax rate of 70% or higher. That rate is absolutely unheard of in any other industry.

> "No deduction or credit shall be allowed for any amount paid or incurred during the taxable year in carrying on any trade or business if such trade or business (or the activities which comprise such trade or business) consists of trafficking in controlled substances (within the meaning of schedule I and II of the Controlled Substances Act) which is prohibited by Federal law or the law of any State in which such trade or business is conducted."

7) Many people who drive this industry are "stoners." While this can be fun, as several business meetings include—or even necessitate—consumption, it also presents unique challenges. Conducting business with people who are under the influence can also be frustrating and managing workplace consumption of Cannabis business employees can be difficult.[34]

---

[33]From a public safety standpoint, it's irresponsible of our government to limit Cannabis entrepreneurs' access to banking. At the time of this writing, the SAFE Banking Act, a bill that would allow Cannabis legal states access to banking has passed in the House of Representatives and is awaiting a vote in the Senate.

[34]For me, stoners is a term of endearment. For some, it is a derogatory term. Context, intent, and impact matter. Also, the industry has become more corporate and this trend will continue as more professionals from other industries transition in and the industry matures.

8) It is often very difficult and sometimes downright illegal to advertise the products around which the industry revolves. Facebook, Google, and most other mainstream marketing channels do not allow the advertisement of a federally illegal narcotic. Even ancillary businesses regularly have their social media accounts, payment processing, and even webhosting shutdown without any prior notice. I myself had my Eventbrite account frozen for hosting events that only discussed Cannabis business. I turned that setback into free PR and additional revenue, more on that in the footnote.[35] It's highly unlikely that you'll see this book advertised on Facebook, as they've banned my account for violating their policies because I was attempting to promote Cannabis education events.

---

[35]One day in 2017, I logged into the High NY Eventbrite account only to discover that my account was suspended. I reached out to customer service and the only response I got was some legal form letter. This was weeks before one of my biggest events, The New York City Cannabis Film Festival. Even though I live in NYC, I am a member of Cannabis education and networking event groups all over the country because I find it's important for me to know what's going on in different regions. I got an email from a Southern California group that also reported they'd been shut down on Eventbrite, even though they, too, organized professional networking events. I called a journalist friend of mine and asked if she wanted an exclusive story. I told her that Eventbrite was purging Cannabis-related accounts, without warning, which was terrible customer service. My business had generated thousands of dollars of ticket service fee revenue for Eventbrite over the years. I was pissed that they banned me without notice. The story was published in Forbes and got a lot of attention. Not only did this help to promote my event and sell more tickets, it also got Eventbrite to respond to my emails right away and reinstate my account almost instantly. Setbacks can turn into opportunities when you creatively apply the high mindset.

9) Industrial Hemp: with over 20,000 documented uses, the non-psychoactive variety of Cannabis has the potential to significantly disrupt the food, energy, plastics, textiles, and paper industries. The infrastructure necessary for this to happen is being built out now. Hemp is the most regenerative crop in the world and can easily change several global business paradigms.

10) The laws and regulations are unpredictable and ever changing. Uncertainty—or risk—is constantly present. Your business can go up in smoke overnight as new regulations get passed and implemented. Just look at what happened in California when adult use legislation went live. Operators had to adjust to new licenses, new rules about packaging, dosage restrictions, allowable pesticides, etc. These are huge changes that require big and often costly pivots that can put a small business out of business.[36] I predict that if and when federal legalization occurs, many state-sanctioned Cannabis businesses will vaporize or combust. More about my predictions for the future of the Cannabis industry in a few chapters.

11) I simply cannot belabor this point enough: the prohibition of Cannabis has been—and continues to be—responsible for

---

[36]There was a deadline for which businesses had to adjust to new regulations to be in compliance. Some edibles brands, for example, had to completely reformulate their products to account for new dosing restrictions and redesign their packaging to conform with new standards. These are processes that can take a lot of time. 4 weeks prior to that deadline, the regulators in some municipalities had yet to announce the regulations. Imagine having less than a month to essentially redesign and repackage your brand, failure meaning a huge fine or losing your license. That could sink a business.

massive, widespread harm and damage to millions of people. In America, communities of color have been the recipients of intergenerational trauma and targeted destruction through Cannabis prohibition. As Amanda Reiman so eloquently pointed out, there are still plenty of people in prison today for minor, Cannabis-related offenses.

The Biggest, Most Important Difference

The legal Cannabis industry and those who benefit from it financially have an imperative, moral obligation to contribute towards healing the people and communities harmed by Cannabis prohibition.

In my humble opinion, it is unethical to profit off the plant without contributing towards reparative measures and restorative actions that benefit the victims of prohibition. I believe all business should be conducted ethically and consciously of its impact on humanity and Mother Earth. In the case of Cannabis business, however, the promise of future profits is built on the brutality of the past.

Turning a blind eye to the collateral consequences of Cannabis prohibition, while commerce in the legal industry is expanding is a complete debasement of Cannabis and a blasphemous act against the mysterious force of Nature that gifted humanity with this prolific and powerful plant. It would be a disgraceful failure to move forward in Cannabis business without prioritizing efforts to repair the harms of prohibition. I will focus much more on this topic in later chapters. For now, it will suffice to say: don't exploit the plant. Instead, leverage its awesomeness to contribute to a higher state of being for humanity. This is not just a feel-good, corporate responsibility buzzword item: nobody in this industry will take you seriously (nor should they) if this isn't one of your core values as a Cannabis business person.

What Action Will You Take Towards Improving the Cannabis Industry?

When I wrote my first book in 2016, this list included another point, the lack of B2B technology and high-tech infrastructure in Cannabis. Thanks to opportunistic entrepreneurs who created businesses like LeafLink, Wurk, Meadow, etc. problems of wholesale transactions, payroll management, and compliant inventory management and point of sale transactions, respectively, now have reliable, scalable technology solutions.[37] Although tech infrastructure is still a work in progress, of all the things on the list, this is the only one in which significant progress has been achieved.[38]

> "Do your homework, this industry is like no other, it really isn't. I've been an analyst for 20 years and I've worked in a variety of industries: technology, energy banking, oil and gas. I mean I've done it all, and truly,

---

[37]The Co-Founders of LeafLink first pitched their business publicly at one of my High NY events that was the only Cannabis event part of Internet Week NYC. A month later, they were in the headlines of TechCrunch for raising a million dollars. They've since grown the business significantly and have raised funding from premier Silicon Alley firm, Lerer Hippeau Ventures.

[38]To be fair, access to capital markets has improved significantly as many corporations have been able to go public in Canada and even be listed on U.S. stock exchanges. However, on the institutional level, the status quo is still very much anti-Cannabis.

there hasn't been one model that I've just been able to take and apply here. So do your research, get as much knowledge and information as possible. This industry is very, very special, it was born from a movement. It's [from] a plant, but it's a plant that has pharmaceutical, recreational, and industrial applications. It's truly diverse."

—Giadha Aguirre De Carcer,[39]
Founder & CEO, New Frontier Data

"Cannabis is unique [compared] to any other industry and it's really important to get to know the culture, to get to know the community, and to get to know the Cannabis. You'd be surprised how many people I've met at industry events who have not smoked before and have a limited understanding of the plant. Whether it's trichomes, the effects, the cannabinoids, if you don't have this language under your belt, it's really hard to engage with people who will take you seriously on the community side. There's a big advocacy component to Cannabis. It's not just about capitalism, it's not just about making money. A lot of people that have been here for a very long time are fighting for decriminalization, for the end of prohibition, for access. Understanding how that plays into being an entrepreneur in this space is important."

—David Hua,
Co-Founder & CEO, Meadow

"This is a very difficult and challenging industry, principally because it's federally illegal. The legality is

---

[39]Giadha and I are both survivors of J.P. Morgan. She spent many more years working there than I did. She's a dynamic, powerful entrepreneur that does first-class business in a first-class way. (J.P.M. inside joke)

happening on the state level; there's no interstate commerce. We have the ever-present banking issue. While the opportunity is significant and long term, the challenges are equally significant. As an entrepreneur you need legal advice from a group of attorneys or counsel that understand the changing legal environment on the state level. There are issues of not being able to deduct normal operating expenses business expenses, so you need accounting and audit advice; this is a dynamic environment. You need to do an extra amount of due diligence and homework. I would recommend engaging help."

—Scott Grieper,
President & Founder, Viridian Capital Advisors

"The Cannabis industry is aging in dog years. Three months [in Cannabis] is equal to about a year in any other [industry]. Things are just evolving and changing so quickly. When I walk into a grow that was built say five years ago, the very early stage stuff that occurred on the East Coast, versus what we're building today, the technology and the style we use now are just night and day different from a few years ago."

—Mark Doherty,[40]
Executive Vice President of Operations, Urban-Gro

"The marijuana industry lies at a unique intersection in American history and politics. In the sense that never before in American history has a movement—created,

---

[40]My mom has attended a few High NY events. Mark was a panelist at one event she attended. My mother was so impressed with Mark she told me after the event that he should be my mentor.

funded, driven largely by people who are interested in the issue because of individual freedom, social justice, good public policy—resulted, almost as a byproduct, in the emergence of a new industry worth billions of dollars a year."

—Ethan Nadelmann,
Founder, Drug Policy Alliance

"We still for many years will be trying to correct the stigma. That's an extra layer of this industry that most people don't understand until they're doing it."

—Danielle Schumacher,
CEO, THC Staffing Group

"If you want to be in this industry, you have to be an activist."

—Ben Pollara,
Founder, LSN Partners[41]

Make no mistake about it. To succeed in Cannabis business, activism is mandatory.

---

[41]Ben was instrumental in running United for Care, the campaign that helped legalize medical Cannabis use in Florida.

9.
Activism Mandatory

"The War on Drugs is a self perpetuating, constantly expanding policy disaster. Every year it's worse than the year before. We've been making it worse now for the last 45 years. We've spent more than $1.5 trillion on this war. All we've got to show for that is this—we've made 50 million arrests for nonviolent drug offenses. Think about that, some countries don't have 50 million people. And we've done everything we can possibly do to destroy the lives of the people we arrest."

—Jack A. Cole,
Founder, Law Enforcement Against Prohibition[42]

"Don't assume it's in the bag. Cannabis isn't going to legalize itself. It's not inevitable. We're in a very real, very tough political battle, and it is far from over."

—Ethan Nadelmann,
Founder, Drug Policy Alliance

Truth, Justice & the Cannabis Way

Attorney Robert Raich, who took two landmark Cannabis cases to the Supreme Court, compares this industry to a rocket ship lifting off. Just a few millimeters off target right now can launch us into the wrong universe 15 or 50 years from now.

How? Because if we don't correct the social injustices of

---

[42]Now known as The Law Enforcement Action Partnership.

prohibition with sensible and fair laws, or, worse, if we allow bad leadership and bad policy to prevail, we can end up in another disastrous situation.

Millions of lives (mostly people of color) have been unjustly harmed and even ruined by Cannabis prohibition.

Who will advocate on behalf of the people with criminal records and limited options to make an honest living? Or those still in jail? Right now, penitentiaries are still full of Cannabis prisoners. According to data from the F.B.I., there were 663,367 marijuana arrests in the U.S. in 2018, more arrests than in 2017. How will those people be made whole?

Who will fight for the sick people who are denied access to safe, natural medicine?

Friend, let it be you. Let it be us.

If not us, then who? If not now, then when?

> "I think every person in this space has an obligation to help people who are still incarcerated or previously incarcerated [for Cannabis] because even when this is completely legal for everybody, there's still going to be people incarcerated for it."
>
> —Danielle Schumacher,
> CEO, THC Staffing Group

When you consider chronic pain, cancer, Alzheimer's, epilepsy, PTSD, MS, etc., there are millions, if not billions, of people around the world who can benefit from the therapeutic use of

Cannabis medicine.[43]

Why then does the U.S. government make it so difficult to research the Cannabis plant's medical properties?

Guess who owns one of the only patents on Cannabinoid medicine in America? I'll give you a hint: it's the U.S. Federal Government. Check out patent number 6630507, which acknowledges "Cannabinoids as antioxidants and neuroprotectants." And yet, as of the writing of this book, Federal policy, via the controlled substances act, maintains that Cannabis has "no accepted medical use." Strange, huh?

What gives the government the right to control what we do with our bodies? Isn't it every human's natural birth right to alter his or her consciousness?

After all, Cannabis is a plant that comes from the Earth.

Imagine if Hemp and its 20,000+ potential uses—superfood, biofuel, clothing, building material, paper, polymer—to name a few, was embraced over the costly, non-renewable resources that it could replace. Hemp is also a natural bioremediation agent, purifying the soil it's grown in, making it a great rotational crop. It's also one of the most effective plants at sequestering carbon dioxide from the air we breathe.

Given all the positive medical and environmental impact this plant is capable of, it's strange that public policy has been so slow

---

[43]I believe every adult human, by the age of 30, has experienced trauma in life. Thus, it stands to reason that the majority of adult humans have some form of post traumatic stress, whether diagnosed or not, and could benefit from Cannabis as part of a holistic treatment plan.

to champion, or even acknowledge, this natural resource.

Rather than waiting for our legislatures to see the light, embrace your civic responsibility and become an agent of change.

Commiting to Cannabis Civics

How do laws get changed in your state?

By ballot initiative or referendum? What legislation has been proposed in your state? Have you voiced your opinions to your elected officials? Is there a local organization educating politicians about Cannabis? Who is helping patients in your community? What are the attitudes of local health care providers?

All politics is local. Start at home.

Change comes from the bottom up. Community boards, city councils, state legislatures, congress members, union leaders, and, of course, donors. These are just some of the characters that play a role in political reform. Being a productive Cannabis citizen requires being a productive citizen. For laws to change and be written in a way that protects Cannabis values, passionate, educated people MUST engage in the political process.

Organizations like NORML, Marijuana Policy Project, Students for Sensible Drug Policy, Americans for Safe Access, Drug Policy Alliance, and Cannabis Voter Project are leading the charge on a national level. On the local level, most Cannabis communities have several groups organizing and advocating on behalf of Cannabis issues.

Find your local groups, get familiar with the work they're doing, and how you can contribute. This is one of the greatest Cannabis investments you can possibly make today. There is no risk and unlimited upside. The only cost is your time and energy. In return, you can expect to expand your Cannabis knowledge base, build your Cannabis network, and be of service to the Cannabis community. All of the above are necessary for success in Cannabis business whether you participate as an operator, investor, or employee.

If you're able to do so, please vote. The 2020 presidential election will be the first one ever where Cannabis is a major issue that candidates must take a stance on. November 2019 polls by Pew and Gallup found support for legalization to be at an all-time high with 67% of Americans in favor.[44]

Don't be fooled by flowery language and campaign promises. Now that Cannabis has broad support from a majority of the U.S. population, politicians are jumping on the bandwagon because they don't want to miss out on the Cannabis vote. This is a unique opportunity to make candidates take positions publicly and to press them for answers to burning questions (like those about economic equity and criminal justice reform). Your vote has power. Make the politicians earn it and hold them accountable for the injustices and bad decisions of their predecessors.

Speaking of accountability, who is paying the lobbyists and greasing the wheels of democracy in your state so that laws are written in a certain way? One reason Cannabis became illegal in

---

[44]https://www.vox.com/policy-and-politics/2019/11/14/20964802/marijuana-legalization-pew-gallup-poll-survey-public-support

the first place was to protect the corporate interests of people who knew that hemp would challenge their empires.[45] To defend the plant and the people who value it will require savvy political participation.

WITHOUT THE WORK OF ACTIVISTS, WHO DROVE THE GRASSROOTS FIGHT FOR CANNABIS FREEDOM, THERE WOULD NOT BE A LEGAL CANNABIS INDUSTRY TODAY.

HONOR THOSE WHO PAVED THE WAY AND STEP UP TO DO YOUR PART.

IF YOU DO NOT CONTRIBUTE TO ACTIVISM, THEN YOU DO NOT DESERVE TO PROFIT FROM CANNABIS LEGALIZATION.

That's not just my opinion. All of the OGs and industry leaders I know agree with me. People who don't agree are not in this book, because I don't affiliate with, nor promote, people who aren't passionate about the bigger picture human rights issues connected to the Cannabis legalization movement.

> "Most of the successful people in the industry right now are interested in this thing beyond money, they're really down for the cause and are

---

[45]Evidence suggests that the original anti-Cannabis campaign of the 1930's was a joint effort by Andrew Mellon, William Randolph Hearst and Pierre Du Pont to protect their business interests in petrochemicals, paper, cotton and nylon, all of which faced serious competition from hemp derived alternatives.

activists."

—Ben Pollara,
Founder, LSN Partners

To be clear, there's nothing wrong with seeking financial gain. However, if you really want to achieve a high level of success in Cannabis, know this: most of the top people are not primarily motivated by money.

Cannabis Business: It's Not For Everyone

If you're not ready to commit to some form of Cannabis activism or advocacy, then this industry might not be for you. At least not right now. And that's OK. It's not for everyone.

I highly encourage you to take a long, hard look inside yourself before you decide to get into the Cannabis industry.

The Cannabis industry is still in a nascent, formative stage. Although there has been unprecedented momentum towards legalization and social acceptance, there is still a long way to go. There's still a huge stigma that exists. There are still many opponents to the mainstreaming of this plant's use and integration into society. Thus, the Cannabis community and its members are subject to higher degrees of scrutiny than professionals in most other industries.

For that reason, anyone who operates in the Cannabis industry automatically becomes an ambassador for the larger Cannabis community. This means you have a higher responsibility to act with integrity and demonstrate to outside observers that not only is Cannabis business safe and productive, but that it also adheres to higher standards of compassion, inclusiveness, and environmental stewardship than other industries.

If business operators and corporate Cannabis citizens fail to do so, there are several groups of organized and well-funded people just waiting for the opportunity to highlight bad behavior to discredit the Cannabis movement. Understand that there are still many people—private prison owners or pharmaceutical company shareholders, for example—who badly want the Cannabis movement to fail. They can hardly wait for the chance to make a big media frenzy about some irresponsible Cannabis entrepreneur being a harmful, bad actor and then using that story to paint the whole industry and community as dangerous. Don't forget how media-driven propaganda helped demonize and stigmatize the plant in the first place.[46]

> "Those of us in the Cannabis business, we need to be stewards of the Cannabis industry. We need to be stewards to our communities and to our government to make sure that the way we act and work with everyone brings the plant up in a good way. We need to practice some altruism and put an industry forth that's the best that it can be, not the greediest it can be."
>
> —Christian Hageseth,
> Founder, Green Man Cannabis and ONE Cannabis Group
> Author of *Big Weed*

Therefore, if you're not ready to hold yourself and your colleagues to the highest possible standards and take ultimate responsibility for each of your actions, then you don't understand

---

[46]William Randolph Hearst's yellow journalism and fear-mongering spread the original anti-"Marihuana" sentiment, calling it "the killer drug" which led to murder, insanity, and death.

the high stakes and bigger picture; and perhaps you're not right for Cannabis business. At least not yet.

And if that's true for you, that's totally cool. No judgement here. But please, if you're not ready to represent the industry wholeheartedly and with complete integrity, then heed Amanda Reiman's advice and wait a few years. There will be space for you.

> "This isn't one of those jobs that you just put away at 5 o'clock and go home, because stigma around Cannabis and Cannabis consumers is everywhere. So if you're going to be in this industry, you have to be willing to speak up at the dinner table when someone says something negative about Cannabis consumers. You have to be willing to go to your child's school when you learn that they're teaching incorrect information about Cannabis and demand that they get the truth. You have to be willing to do these things. I don't mean to sound callous, but if you're not willing to do those things, don't be in the industry right now. Wait. Wait 5 years, 10 years when Cannabis is just like alcohol and working in Cannabis doesn't mean you're stigmatized and you don't need to be this big defender. Then, get into the industry. Right now we need people that are gonna push us forward and not people that are gonna weigh us down."
>
> —Amanda Reiman, PhD
> Director of Community Relations, Flow Kana

Do The Right Thing

> "Being involved in activism and advocacy around

Cannabis is tremendously important. To know that there is a large picture here and the progress that [we're] making is built off the backs of activists and advocates that did it without expecting a payout at the end of the day. They did it because it was the right thing to do."

—Kayvan Khalatbari,
Founding Partner, Denver Relief, Denver Relief Consulting
Board of Directors, Minority Cannabis Business Association

A commitment to activism demonstrates a commitment to Cannabis culture and an interest in the industry that extends beyond financial gain.

Over the course of my interviews, many of the leaders expressed that they prefer to work with people who are in Cannabis business for "the right reasons." More on that below:

"If you're going to get involved in this industry, make sure you really care and that you're doing this for the right reasons. This is such an emerging industry and it's [built] on the backs of people who spent years and years toiling away in advocacy and activism for very little money. People have sacrificed a lot more than I have. People have gone to jail for doing exactly what people are now making real money doing—never lose sight of that. This is not just a regular business. We have a much larger moral obligation to do this the right way... Because if we don't, the whole thing can come crashing down and all those years of work and toil and sweat and labor that we've all put in to try and get to this point could be for naught. Just because some folks decided they wanted to cut corners or ship stuff out the back door or use some of the same sort of shady business tactics that we see [in other industries]. The Cannabis industry is highly scrutinized. This industry is driving culture right now. Operators and entrepreneurs are representing the industry at large and the community at large."

—Kris Krane,[47]
Co-Founder and President, 4Front Ventures

"I refuse to believe that anything that's innovative is so at the cost of the environment. So, from a personal and ethical standpoint I like to invest in [businesses] that are sustainable. Furthermore, it's critical to the bottom line of Cannabis businesses for them to be sustainable."

—Emily Paxhia,
Founding Partner, Poseidon Asset Management

If you're looking to get hired in the Cannabis industry and, like most people, don't have formal Cannabis experience, activist work demonstrates passion and commitment for the plant. When I spoke at the inaugural Vegas Cannabis Summit, I met with the operators of the first few licensed adult use dispensaries in Las Vegas. Across the board, they agreed that candidates with activism experience on their resumes automatically had a leg up against candidates without it.

---

[47]Long before Kris became a Cannabis business leader, he contributed to activism in a major way for many years with tenures as Associate Director of NORML and Executive Director of SSDP.

10.
Business as Usual

Now that we've gone over the most important Cannabis business decisions, defined success in a SMART way, identified the 10 characteristics of highly successful Cannabis entrepreneurs, examined how the Cannabis industry is unlike any other, and acknowledged that activism is mandatory, let's get down to the business of Cannabis business.

What is an entrepreneur? There are plenty of definitions I can offer, but none can truly capture the dynamic nature of the role: inventor, artist, gambler, self-disciplinarian, alchemist. One thing I can tell you with absolute certainty is this: entrepreneurship is a seriously challenging yet rewarding craft to practice.

Entrepreneurship is a way of life.

It's a mindset manifested through powerful habits, expressed with integrity through energetic execution, all built on a foundation of values, beliefs, and commitment to a higher purpose.

And it's even more difficult in the Cannabis industry.

Many of the leaders I interviewed agreed that Cannabis isn't the best industry for first-time entrepreneurs. Why? Largely due to the industry's regulatory and operational complexity, an unpredictable and shifting legal environment, and the rapid rate of innovation. Beyond that, the Cannabis business world is full of wily characters, opportunistic scammers, hardened criminals, and all kinds of sharks who are just ready to eat fools alive.

> Despite the vast amount of opportunities and the money that's out there, there's a lot of competition...and some people don't play nice."
>
> —Andrew DeFries, PhD
> Founder, 710 Vermont

When I asked Cannabis business leaders for advice for first-time Cannabis entrepreneurs, many offered the same answer: "Don't do it." Some were half joking, some were completely serious. Others, like Steve DeAngelo, said they'd give Cannabis entrepreneurs the same advice they'd give any type of entrepreneur because, at the core of it all, business fundamentals are the same across any industry.

That being said, it's absolutely possible to succeed in Cannabis without prior entrepreneurship experience. That's exactly what Nial DeMena did.

The Green American Dream

Against all odds, Nial seized the opportunity to become the green American dream.

Raised in Maine by a financially-strapped single mother, Nial's journey is rooted in humble beginnings. Growing up, Nial excelled in athletics and academics, enjoying the meritocracy and constant challenge offered in both arenas. He credits his years playing varsity sports and serving as team captain for developing his leadership skills. Eventually, he earned himself a scholarship and went to college as an English major.

After graduating college, Nial worked as a private tutor and completed a Master's degree in Rhetoric and Technical Writing. Not exactly the credentials you'd expect for an entrepreneur who would go on to build a multi-million dollar Cannabis enterprise.

Shortly after Massachusetts legalized medical use of Cannabis in 2012, Nial was encouraged by his girlfriend's father to look into the Cannabis industry. Nial's then girlfriend, now wife, Julia Germaine, had a Bachelor's degree in Plant Biology and a Master's in Poetry. Julia's father had recently sold his business in the medical field, and was a big believer in the virtues of medical Cannabis. He encouraged the young couple—still in their mid-twenties—to take a chance on the emerging industry, which he saw as having unlimited potential.

Intrigued by an opportunity they viewed as democractic, meritocratic, and with unlimited upside, Julia and Nial began working on an application for a medical Cannabis dispensary. It didn't take long until the duo began impressing local elected officials and stakeholders with their professionalism and commitment to excellence.

According to Nial, "We didn't really know what we were doing, we were just trying our best. When we started getting external validation from experienced and influential people, we knew that we were onto something and that just made us more motivated to succeed."

Despite having the highest scoring application in their municipality, due to the political nature of Cannabis licensure, the couple was not awarded a license. They were devastated, but not defeated.

This seemingly failed experiment provided them with experience and relationships they used to explore other Cannabis business opportunities. As the regulatory landscape shifted in Massachusetts, Nial and Julia consulted for another team that had an experience similar to theirs in a different municipality. Together, this combined team would go on to win 3 dispensary licenses in Massachusetts.

Nial, in true visionary fashion, was already anticipating success and planning ahead. He understood that winning a license was just the beginning. So Nial began thinking about how to differentiate a dispensary by offering unique products. It was around that time Nial had the inspiration for what would become the cornerstone of his 8-figure enterprise.

Leveraging his background in technical writing, Nial devoured scientific studies to learn about different mechanisms through which medicine can be delivered. He was particularly intrigued with transdermal patches, something that did not exist in the world of Cannabis. In a non-traditional industry like Cannabis, a non-traditional background can be a tremendous asset.[48]

"My ability to dive into deeply technical fields, hybridize knowledge, and communicate complex concepts in a simple, understandable way is what allowed me to recruit others and get them excited about my vision," Nial explained.

---

[48]There really is no "traditional" or typical Cannabis background yet. That means no matter who you are, you can fit into the industry.

Seeing the opportunity to create a new category of Cannabis products, Nial who had never previously raised venture capital, approached his two Cannabis consulting clients and asked for seed funding. Both said yes and Manna Molecular Science was born.

Rather than reinventing the patch, Nial took advantage of his proximity to MIT, Harvard, and the Massachusetts biotech and pharma ecosystem to identify and recruit one of the world's leading experts on pharmaceutical transdermal patches to design his products.

Since 2015, Manna Molecular has launched products in over a dozen markets, has consecutively doubled its revenues for the past 3 years, and is on pace to generate 8 figures of revenue in 2020.

In 2019, continuing in the spirit of innovation, Nial recruited Dr. Harin Padma-Nathan, who oversaw clinical trials of Viagra and Cialis, to join Manna in developing a Cannabinoid-based gel designed to help women with challenges of sexual dysfunction. Manna expects this product to hit the market in 2020. I joked with Nial that his legacy would be to help millions of women around the world orgasm.

All kidding aside, Nial credits his success to the world class talent on his team and the encouragement he received from his mentors. The people closest to him pushed him to forge his own path and strive for greatness in a nascent industry where he would not be limited by his resume, a perceived lack of credentials, or a glass (or grass) ceiling. That is the beauty of Cannabis business. This industry is still in the early stages of development and there's plenty of room for innovators to create massive impact.

So in case nobody has told you yet, let me be the one to say that you can do what Nial did. Allow his story to inspire you and remind you that a first-time entrepreneur can create an 8-figure business in just a few years. That opportunity exists for you in Cannabis business. Have no doubt, the Green American Dream is real and it's possible.

Entrepreneurship Education

Entrepreneurship is a dance: there are rules, routines, rhythms, and plenty of room for improvisation. Whether you're talking about Cannabis, cotton candy, or corn flakes, Capitalism follows certain fundamental rules: supply and demand, competition, free cash flows, intellectual property, customer service. These aren't just concepts or buzzwords, these are realities that every entrepreneur must continuously be cognizant of.

The art and science of entrepreneurship goes back many generations. We are phenomenally lucky to live in the information age, where knowledge is easier to access than ever before. Thanks to books and the internet, you can dive into some of the greatest business minds of all time all from the comfort of your home. If you don't know anything about entrepreneurship, take some classes, read some books, and find a mentor who can help you.

Educate yourself, but make no mistake about it, entrepreneurship is about strategic action. You don't learn to dance by reading books about dance. To truly #entrepreneur, you must be willing to boldly step out and leave it all on the dance floor.

Here are some questions for you to seriously consider before starting any business venture, whether it's Cannabis related or not.

- Who is your target customer and how are you providing value to them? Be as specific as possible. Specialize and find a niche. Don't try to be everything for everyone, that's a sure-fire way to fail in spectacular fashion.
- Does your product or service already exist? Why or why not?
- What problem does your business solve? How important (valuable) is solving that problem and for whom? How urgent is it for that problem to be solved? How are people currently solving that problem? What evidence do you have to support your answers to the above questions?
- How can you test your answers to the above questions in a low risk, cost-effective manner to validate your beliefs?
- How much will it cost to create your product or service? What suppliers, partners, or key resources do you need to make your product or deliver your service? Will there be enough profit margin to justify the work?
- How will you market and sell your products or services?
- How does your business scale?
- What's the total available market (TAM)?[49] How long will it take to penetrate that market?
- What's the serviceable available market (SAM)?[50] How

---

[49]Total market demand for a product or service, sometimes defined as Total Available Market.

[50]The segment of the TAM which is within your geographical reach.

much of that SAM can you win and how will you do it?[51]

- How will you protect your market share or differentiate your business?

To put it bluntly, how will your business make money?

If these questions sound like no-brainers for you—great! Take action to test the answers you've come up with. If these questions aren't ones you've even considered, then you'd be wise to invest time and energy in educating yourself about the magical crafts and high sciences of business and entrepreneurship. Note: it will take a long time to independently gain the necessary experience and know-how to start and successfully run a business.

Imagine if you were tasked with building a bridge and given all the tools, materials, instructions, and schematics necessary to get the job done. Could you build that bridge? Do you think you'd build it faster, with greater integrity, and more ease if you had a professional bridge builder guiding you through the process?

Would you want a few good master craftsmen, architects, and engineers on your team? Having a team to delegate to and share the workload with enables greater efficiency and effectiveness. It also creates more checkpoints for quality control and accountability, decreasing the likelihood of critical errors.

Business is a team sport. Working with a business coach or experienced mentor can help you achieve in one year what might

---

Sometimes called Serviceable Available Market.

[51]The answer to this question is sometimes referred to as SOM, Serviceable Obtainable Market or Share of Market.

otherwise take you several years or even a lifetime on your own. Working as an apprentice or intern to a master ganjapreneur is another great way to learn the (hemp) ropes of this industry.

When I served as a Cannabis industry mentor to the National Science Foundation's iCorp entrepreneurship development training program, one of the main resources we used in the training of new entrepreneurs was the Business Model Canvas. This is one of my favorite frameworks for designing and analyzing business models. I highly recommend this tool to all entrepreneurs, but especially to those running Cannabis businesses where market dynamics change quickly and pivots happen frequently.

If you've already got the fundamentals of business down, and even if you don't, commit yourself to getting a world-class Cannabis education.

Cannabis Education

How much do you know about the Cannabis plant?

- Have you grown it? Have you purchased it?
- Have you consumed it?
- Have you sold it?
- Do you know how it became illegal?
- Do you know about the endocannabinoid system, the biological mechanisms through which Cannabis impacts humans and animals?
- How come Cannabis seems to effectively treat so many different diseases?
- What does it mean to get high?

- Is Cannabis dangerous?
- Can you tell safe, clean, quality Cannabis products from dirty and dangerous ones?
- What's the difference between Cannabis and Hemp?
- What is Hemp used for?
- How do edibles work?
- What are terpenes?
- What's a dab?
- How much does it cost to make a pound of Cannabis?[52]

If you don't have immediate, solid answers to most of the above questions, then you need to develop your Cannabis acumen. And even if you do, you need to continually expand your Cannabis knowledge as new discoveries occur.

There are several resources you can make use of to increase your Cannabis IQ. Here are some of my recommendations:

- Americans for Safe Access
- *Cannabis: A Beginner's Guide to Growing Marijuana* by Dan Danko
- *The Cannabis Encyclopedia* by Jorge Cervantes
- *The Cannabis Pharmacy* by Michael Backes
- Clover Leaf University
- Drug Policy Alliance
- Freedom Leaf

---

[52]This is a trick question. It depends on the quality, production methods, and type of finished product. For example, a pound of indoor vs. outdoor flower will have different production costs on different sized farms. Industrial hemp and high THC flower have different prices. Producing a pound of concentrated Cannabis extract will vary in cost based on the extraction method and the quality of Cannabis from which it was derived. I can buy a pound of organic hemp seeds to put into my morning oatmeal on Amazon.com for $15… if I planted those seeds in my backyard, what would happen?

- Green Flower Media (try promo code **GFLOVE25**)
- *Healing With CBD* by Eileen Konieczny and Lauren Wilson
- *Hemp Bound* by Doug Fine
- Leafly
- *Marijuana Grower's Handbook* & *Beyond Buds* by Ed Rosenthal
- MarijuanaMoment.net
- Marijuana Policy Project
- NORML
- Oaksterdam University
- ProjectCBD.org
- Search for academic journal articles on Google Scholar, JSTOR
- Students for Sensible Drug Policy
- *The Cannabis Manifesto* by Steve DeAngelo
- *The Emperor Wears No Clothes* by Jack Herer
- *The Marijuana Manifesto* by Jesse Ventura
- WeedWeek

Learn from experienced people. Go to conferences, trade shows, meetups, and all sorts of high functions. Read books, articles, newsletters. Get to know the people and, especially, the plant that make this industry happen. The plant is at the core of it all, and there's a lot to learn about it.

Amber Senter, the Founder and CEO of Leisure Life Products, a line of Cannabis infused product brands in Oakland, C.A., told me the best investment she ever made was, "learning [about] the Cannabis plant itself. There were several years before I actually entered the industry where I just studied the plant. Everything about the plant. How it grows, how to clone it, how to trim it, how to cure it, all the things. Almost obsessively studying Cannabis."

Now, in addition to owning several Cannabis product brands,

Amber is also Co-Founder and Executive Director of Supernova Women, a non-profit that empowers women of color to lead in the Cannabis industry. She also lobbies for more equitable Cannabis laws in California.

The bottom line is this: investing in your Cannabis education is one of the best investments you can make. Doing so will empower you to take advantage of opportunities in the industry and increase your likelihood of succeeding in Cannabis business.

Thinking you can succeed in Cannabis business without an extensive underlying knowledge of the Cannabis plant is at best arrogant and foolish. At worst, it can be deadly.

In 2019, more than 40 people in the U.S. died due to vape-related injuries. They were victims of irresponsible, illegal operators who didn't have enough science and Cannabis knowledge to understand that they were creating dangerous products. Or they were so greedy and willing to cut corners for profit that they didn't care about the safety of their products.

Do you want to consume Cannabis products made by people lacking sufficient Cannabis knowledge? I don't, and I don't want anyone else to either.

If you intend to make Cannabis your profession, then be a pro by cultivating the highest possible level of Cannabis education.

11.
The 5 Most Common Cannabis Business Mistakes To Avoid

The #1 most common Cannabis business mistake is not only the most frequent cause of failure for Cannabis entrepreneurs, but it's also the most dangerous (and most avoidable) mistake of them all, that's why it's #1.

I alluded to it in previous chapters, it's a mistake I made; if you were paying attention, likely you already know what it is.

The #1 most common Cannabis business mistake is not doing enough research about what you're getting yourself into and not planning adequately before starting your Cannabis business.

> "Do your research, [that's] number one. Take time to understand what it is you're jumping into. This is particularly true if you're new to Cannabis as well as to the Cannabis industry. Be flexible if you're coming into Cannabis from any other industry—the strategies and techniques that you used to be successful in other places should inform what you do with Cannabis [business] but don't rely on them. It's very, very different and so the only thing that you can really be sure of in the Cannabis industry is that something will happen that you weren't expecting and there's a lot of independent variables so you need to be both flexible and resilient."
>
> —Steve DeAngelo,
> Co-Founder, Harborside Dispensary Group,

"The first step is reading and learning who the key players are, look at what they're up to. Next is understanding the regulatory landscape of the Cannabis industry, which is super important when investing because all the different markets have different rules. And if you're not living and breathing it every day, and you're not engaging in those markets, you're likely not on top of how to capture the inefficiencies in the markets through what I like to title "regulatory arbitrage", which is the difference in rules between markets. Get educated, read everything, study market data, get to know authentic people in the industry. Find a niche where you can add clear demonstrable value, get really good at it, and then be known for it. Focus."

—Asher Troppe,
CEO & Co-Founder, Tress Capital

"[Before getting involved,] I spent almost seven months researching the industry, traveling to different states, I met with some governors of states that legalized, I met with my relationships at the DEA in a couple of states, I visited my first grows and dispensaries. Bloomberg ranks [Cannabis] as one of the fastest growing industries in the world. But it is still very much a collegial marketplace. There's a core group of people in it, and I think it's important to dive in and become an insider to really get a feel for, not only where the industry is today, where it's going, but what got the industry here. Because it's been a very long fight. You've really got to get yourself inside the evolution of the advocacy for social change, the advocacy that's developed the different state balloting and legalization efforts that got us to where we are. That is the root of the business opportunity in Cannabis. It started decades ago, and I think to really understand where this industry is going, you've got to have some sense of where it's come from."

—Scott Grieper,
President & Founder, Viridian Capital Advisors

"When I was in my twenties, back in the 1980s, I was learning everything I possibly could about drugs and drug policy. I was a graduate student and I just spent endless hours in the libraries reading the articles, reading the books, I got myself fellowships, and interviewed DEA agents around the world. That investment of spending years learning the issue [was the best investment I ever made], and the outcome was that when I finally was ready to start teaching and speaking and writing in the late 80s, my level of confidence was very high and I had something to say."

—Ethan Nadelmann,
Founder, Drug Policy Alliance

"If you're going to be in this industry, I think you'll be most successful if you truly understand the inner workings of prohibition. There's a lot of trauma, not just for people in this industry but also for consumers. If you don't understand that, you won't be speaking to your consumer, and so you won't be successful... Get an education and understand what the last 50 years of Cannabis policy has looked like in the United States (and beyond)."

—Amanda Reiman, PhD
Director of Community Relations, Flow Kana

"Have an idea of what to expect. Don't expect it to be the easiest, coolest job you've ever had. Most people I know in this industry are working just as hard or harder than they'd be working in other jobs. There are extra levels of stress due to uncertainty with how things are defined and with [all the] sudden changes."

—Danielle Schumacher
CEO, THC Staffing Group

Cannabis is a risky business. Do yourself a favor and do your homework before embarking on the Cannabis entrepreneur's journey. Otherwise, expect to learn some painful lessons.

If you're reading this book, you're already doing some research before diving in. It's good to dip your toe in first and test the waters. Nobody's ever drowned that way.

What's Your One Thing?

The second most common mistake I discovered in my personal experience as both a Cannabis entrepreneur and Cannabis business coach is lack of focus or specialization.

Not surprisingly, one of the most common pieces of advice industry leaders gave was this: pick one thing and do it really well, better than anybody else. Don't try to do everything. Cannabis is too big. There's too much ground to cover.

As an investor, Owner, SVP, and Chief Mentor at the Arcview Group, Francis Priznar reviews over 1,500 Cannabis business investment pitches and mentors about 100 Cannabis business founders every year. He told me that focus is the greatest challenge for Cannabis entrepreneurs: "I think there's excessive concern about legal risk in Cannabis. I know the risk is there, of course, let's not ignore it. However, the chance of the business failing due to poor management is much greater than that for legal compliance, so staying focused on the business is crucial...Too many people in the Cannabis industry are all over the place."

> "Focus. You have to learn to pass up opportunities. There isn't enough time, resources, and money to effectively pursue all of them."
>
> —Kris Krane,
> Co-Founder and President, 4Front Ventures

In his book, *Zero to One*, Peter Thiel of Founders Fund, co-founder of PayPal, early investor in Facebook, and early investor in Privateer Holdings, makes the claim that the best companies are small monopolies. Build your small monopoly in some niche and defend it. Create something that will generate predictable revenue. To do so, you must be consistent in the product or service your business provides. You must have impeccable customer service and a commitment to excellence. Remember, this is an industry built around compassion.

In the Cannabis industry, the challenge is not finding opportunity, but rather remaining focused on one long enough to bring it to fruition as new ones are constantly emerging. There is so much opportunity in Cannabis that eager entrepreneurs often claim (or make the excuse) that their greatest challenge is having too many to choose from.

Discipline is required to stick with one idea long enough to see it through and reap the benefits. What you say "No" to is as important as what you say "Yes" to. Before making commitments or taking on new risks, think about your long-term vision and whether or not the proposed actions bring you closer to or further from your end goal. Don't get spread thin and become ineffective as a result.

From a branding standpoint, it's a lot easier for your customers, fans, and partners to talk about you if they know you for one thing. For example, the brand Raw is synonymous with rolling papers. Make it easy for others to share your brand and your identity in the marketplace. How? By keeping it simple and doing one thing really well.

Play the Long Game

Rome wasn't built in a day. Neither was the Internet. The legal Cannabis industry is no different. Many industry insiders agree that the end of Federal Cannabis Prohibition is at least a few years away. It will then take another 5 – 15 years for all the regulatory frameworks to be ironed out. If you're viewing Cannabis as a get-rich-quick opportunity, think again.

Yes, the opportunities are immediate, but please don't enter this industry with a Gordon Gecko, "Greed is good" approach. That's not what the Cannabis community is about. The payouts might not come for a while, and the amount of challenges along the way are guaranteed to be significant. If you're not in it to create a better world through the healthier integration of Cannabis into everyday life, then you should think again about entering the Green Rush. Perhaps you're making mistake #1.

Be honest with yourself.

> "It's going to be a long play no matter what you do if you want to do it right. There's a lot of people who come in and think that you can make a quick buck, but in reality, you really can't. It's very difficult to do that—you have banking issues, you have high legal costs, different regulatory issues you need to be concerned with. So unless you're doing something ancillary, it's definitely going to be a long-term thing that you need to be prepared for."
>
> —Evan Nison,[53]
> Founder & CEO, NisonCo PR
> Co-Founder, Whoopi & Maya

> "I see a lot of people pop into the industry, make a big splash, and six months later they're literally nowhere to be found. They take a lot of time and energy away from other people who are trying to focus on taking care of patients and on legalization. I think they do themselves and the industry a great disservice."
>
> —Christie Lunsford,
> CEO, The Hemp Biz Conference

If you regularly attend certain annual trade shows, you'll notice exactly what Christie is talking about. One year you see a company spending thousands of marketing dollars on a booth, and by next year's show they're out of business. She credits this

---

[53]Evan walks the walk. He's one of the most influential and successful millennials in Cannabis. He's the youngest member of the NORML Board of Directors and sits on the Board of Directors of Students for Sensible Drug Policy. He's been an activist leader for a decade and has run successful businesses in the industry for several years.

to people's inability to pace themselves. If you're not thinking long term, it's going to be really hard to pace yourself. This is especially true given how quickly the Cannabis industry changes and how simultaneously slowly institutional, culture-wide reform happens. Being an entrepreneur in this industry is like sprinting a super-marathon. I'm not telling you that to intimidate you, but rather to help avoid making mistake #1.

If there's anyone who is qualified to speak on Cannabis endurance, it's Christie Lunsford. She's a versatile Cannabis industry veteran who has just about done it all. In 2017, while working as the COO of an LED lighting and grow-tech company, she served on the Board of Directors for the National Cannabis Industry Association. For years, her consulting business advised Cannabis business license applicants across the nation. At the December 2015 Cannabis Business Awards, Christie was awarded the first Cannabis Woman of the Year Award. Prior to that, she developed some of the original intellectual property and formulations that became the basis for Dixie Elixirs, the Colorado-based infused products brand. Most recently, Christie has been producing The Hemp Biz Conference all over the nation. And she has done all of that on top of being a mother.

When I met Christie, the way she treated me made me feel like I was her son. Warmth, compassion, and gentle support just flow out of her. No doubt, it was that same grounded, motherly energy that Christie provided to medical patients when she was a caregiver in the early days of Colorado's medical Cannabis program. Given how profound her Cannabis business resume is, Christie's humility continually inspires me.

Shortly after Pennsylvania passed legislation to establish a medical Cannabis program, an artist friend whom I had only known as a big chiefer and super maven of rap and reefer surprised me.[54] He let me know he was part of an investor group—his family had some successful and influential entrepreneurs in it—that was interested in pursuing Pennsylvania medical licenses. He asked for my help to get the project going. And so I recommended and introduced Christie (as well as a few other) folks to set my friend up for success.

Before meeting with Christie, my friend did some Googling and was skeptical because he judged Christie by her appearance, claiming she looked like a midwestern soccer mom who'd probably never gotten high in her Life. "What could this white lady possibly know about weed?" he asked. I assured him not to judge a book by its cover and that Christie was as real as it gets. After one introductory meeting, the group was ready to retain her for consultation. My friend, the artist, and his team of sharks were impressed by Christie's rare combination of competence, sincerity, and kindness. Thanks for your leadership Christie!

> "It changes faster than any other industry out there."
>
> —Giadha Aguirre De Carcer,
> Founder & CEO, New Frontier Data

> "Things are changing every day. Tons of new entrants to all angles of the industry, every day."
>
> —Asher Troppe,
> CEO & Co-Founder, Tress Capital

The 3 previous mistakes will kill your business slowly. The next 2

---

[54]Rap and reefer are two of my favorite art forms and a classic combination.

will put you on the fast track to failure: #4 is partnering with bad people and #5 is not learning from mistakes—yours and those made by others. The mistakes discussed in this chapter are largely avoidable. However, if you make the most common Cannabis business mistake, being underprepared, then you're very likely to make mistakes numbers #2 – #5 as well.

As a quick and significant counterpoint, know that you will rarely, if ever, feel 100% prepared to take a big risk like entering the Cannabis business or starting your own company. Don't let perfection become the enemy of execution. Do your diligence, assess your risks, trust your gut, and take a leap of faith when you feel 75% or 80% ready. You may never feel 100% ready, so don't deprive yourself of a bigger opportunity because of your fear, doubt, or uncertainty. To be ready, you must simply decide that you're ready. Then, get set and go.

To recap, the top 5 Cannabis mistakes to avoid are:

1. Insufficient planning, research, and preparation

2. Lack of focus, specialization and clear SMART goals

3. Thinking short term instead of playing the long game

4. Partnering with the wrong people

5. Not learning from mistakes

12.

Raising Capital For Your Cannabis Business

Despite my humanistic—and borderline hippie ideals—I understand that we live in a world dominated by Capitalism. Discussing Cannabis business without covering the topic of capital would be like trying to roll a joint without paper.

Businesses simply cannot exist without mechanisms for attracting and deploying financial and human capital.

Let's start with money.

New money is entering the Cannabis industry every day. In 2018, more institutional investors entered the industry than ever before. Many Cannabis companies got listed on the NASDAQ and other major exchanges, and Canada legalized adult use on the federal level. International trade expanded as more countries adopted legalization.

In 2019, this trend continued as more than $11 billion investment dollars entered the Cannabis industry.[55]

Below, in no particular order, are 5 fundamental categories that any professional investor will evaluate before giving your Cannabis startup a red cent or green paper.

These are also criteria that potential partners or employees will

---

[55] Source: Viridian Deal Tracker 12/13/19

evaluate as well, if they're savvy:

Human Capital or Team

- Who is on the team and what is the team's chemistry like?
- What experience do they have in business and entrepreneurship?
- Are they trustworthy, fully committed, and coachable?
- What makes them uniquely qualified to win?
- Who is the leader and do they lead effectively?
- Does the investor get along with the core team members on a personal level?
- Is this team prepared to scale, pivot, or evolve, and what might that look like?
- How much money, time, and effort has the team invested in the business?
- What's the quality of corporate governance? Do they have experienced Cannabis attorneys and accountants behind them?

Value Proposition

- What problem does your product or service solve?
- What are the target customer segments, how well do you understand them, and how large is each?
- How important or expensive is the problem you're solving for the customer segments you're targeting?
- Are the target customers willing to spend money on a solution to that problem you've identified?
- How are your target customers currently solving the problem?

- What data do you have to validate the answers to the above questions?
- What unique value does your business offer that nobody else can easily duplicate? Or what sets your solution apart from other solutions?
- Is the timing right for your solution, product, or service? How do you know?

Business Model

- What are the unit economics of implementing your product or service? How did you arrive at those numbers?
- What are the revenue streams and the cost structures associated with your business?
- How does it scale? How can you build a system to consistently and predictably monetize the product or service?
- Have you detailed and enumerated the risks, threats, and competitors to your business?
- What gaps or weaknesses do you need to fill?
- What differentiates your model? Is it defensible or can a competitor easily copy it? Do you have proprietary intellectual property?
- Through what channels will you attract, acquire, and retain customers?
- What key partners, resources, and activities define your business? How much experience do you have with the above?
- What are the capital requirements to launch and continue operating your business?

- What additional capital needs might the business have, if any?

Understanding of Cannabis Industry Dynamics

- Do you know the industry players? How well?
- Can you speak intelligently about the competitive landscape and industry current events?
- What unique insight do you have about your target customers, how they operate, and what their decision-making process is like?
- In what direction do you see the marketplace heading? Based on what?
- How will your company adapt to and deal with uncertainty?
- What systematic, regulatory, or industry specific risks are you vulnerable to?
- What do you know or believe that nobody else in the industry does?

Exit & R.O.I.

- What are the terms & conditions for the investment that you seek?[56]
- How are you going to use the funds?
- What is the plan for exit?
- What does a successful exit look like? Who (if any) are the potential acquirers?

---

[56]If you aren't well versed in venture finance, I recommend reading a book like _Venture Deals_ so you understand and can speak to the various ways deals are structured, how valuations works, and the terms that matter most to ensure that you protect your financial interests in your business.

- What are the benchmarks, key performance indicators, and milestones that need to be met along the way?
- How long will it take to make the investor's money back? How long to generate a return on investment?
- What return are you planning to generate for your investors?

How To Get An Investor To Say Yes And Cut A Check

Have all the answers for the above questions squared away and you've got a fighting chance.

> "It comes down to management. In an emerging industry, it always comes down to management. I prefer to work with management teams that have successfully started, scaled, funded, grown, and exited businesses. The whole round trip. I prefer teams who have experience in early stage markets...Within that, I look for someone on the management team with experience in heavily-regulated industries because that's what Cannabis is."
>
> —Scott Grieper,
> President & Founder of Viridian Capital Advisors

> "Almost a deal breaker: solo founders. I really like having 2 or 3 co-founders. Starting a business is really, really, really hard work. And I feel happy knowing that there's more than 1 person thinking about it 24 hours a day and working together."
>
> —Alain Bankier,
> Founding Partner, New York Angels

> "The first thing is the team. So if the team doesn't seem like they're going to be a good fit for [our] values, I think

that that's a big deal breaker...I do not like to work with people who demonstrate hubris to the point where it puts them at a weakness in running their business...Another barrier is unwillingness to take things seriously around the operations, such as financial controls or really thinking about how this is going to go to market. Those things are really big barriers. And then we just we have a standard due diligence checklist, so if something doesn't make it through that in general we're probably not going to make the investment."

—Emily Paxhia,
Founding Partner, Poseidon Asset Management

When it comes to raising private capital for your business, often the first thing the investor will assess are the humans operating the business. And as Alain Bankier pointed out, if you're a solopreneur looking to raise private capital, expect to have a difficult time. Investors want to mitigate risk, and for them to know that there are several competent, motivated people working together on creating ROI is more comforting than knowing that the safety of their investment relies on only one person.

One of the most common mistakes I've seen entrepreneurs make when fundraising is not being clear and deliberate enough about their ask. Indeed, the professional investors I interviewed all complained about entrepreneurs with unrealistic valuations, unreasonably optimistic projections, and asking for inappropriate amounts of capital.

Understanding the Investor's Mindset

"An investor's job is to manage and mitigate risk."

—Kenny Dichter,
CEO, Wheels Up

Imagine if you had millions or billions of dollars to invest. In between travelling the world and enjoying the finer things, you look for ways to make money with your money. It sounds nice, huh? What kind of person would you like to bet on? List out the character traits of that ideal person, or think about people in your life you'd trust with a large sum of your hard-earned (or fortunately-inherited) money. What are those people like? Do you share those qualities? If not, what can you do to practice or develop those traits?

Investors—the good ones, like all serious business people—are very intentional about where they place their time and money. When you have enough money that you're able to put lots of it to work and take on big financial risks, it's likely you value your time, a scarce resource, much more than your money, an abundant one.

Here's how investors will typically evaluate your business. Within the blink of an eye, investors (and most humans) will form a first impression and judgement of you. On the binary scale, they will decide they either like and trust you enough to receive your pitch or they don't. Assuming they do, they aren't going to dive into the details of your business plan with a fine tooth comb. Instead, they will ask for the very brief, high-level pitch, an elevator pitch, or the summary of your business model, which should include something uniquely juicy about what makes your business special.

Investors get down to business. If they like the pitch, they will ask what the terms of the offer are. What are you selling (equity, debt, warrants, etc.), how much are you asking for, and why? I cannot stress this enough: you have to have a precise, realistic strategy about what you plan to do with the money. This needs to be as concise, clear, and easily digestible as the rest of your elevator pitch. And the end goal must be profit or return oriented. It's ok to ask for a range and, certainly, negotiating terms is part of the process. There's a courtship element at play in fundraising. Just know that you better have a good, logical justification for your ask.

Take a look at how the following statements leave different impressions:

"I need cash to grow the business. A million bucks would be great. How much you got?"

"We're seeking $100,000 in seed funding for a 10% equity stake."

"We're offering 10% equity for $100,000 that will allow us to build betas, test them with our target customers with whom we already have LOIs, and then in 6 – 12 months, after incorporating their feedback, we will be seeking a $1,000,000 Series A to go to market with a finished product."

The first example would probably put off any investor. The second would demonstrate a basic competence and invite some questions. The third indicates thoughtfulness, thoroughness, and invites more pointed questions.

Once you make your ask/offer, the investor will then, if interested, ask for more information and begin his or her diligence process. And that's when you will actually get grilled, so prepare to have every aspect of your business (and team) scrutinized, examined, and evaluated. Assuming the investor is sold on you, your team, and your business, then, before the deal gets done, it will go to the investor's legal team and perhaps their financial advisors as well. Expect terms to be negotiated and expect further scrutiny from the investor's team.

Do not think of these questions and inspections as obstacles. Striving to meet an investor's disciplined standards will force you to think more deeply about your business than you might ever have before. And it will save you from making critical errors as your venture grows. Embrace the process.

Accountants and attorneys, by the way, are great resources for capital raising. Every wealthy person I know—and certainly every professional investor I've ever met—works with at least one and often with several lawyers and accountants. Not only do these service providers have a network of wealthy potential financiers for your Cannabis venture, but they also are likely to have the trust that only comes with an established business relationship.

Above all else: always be honest, respectful, and appreciative of the time a potential investor is giving you. Even if they say no, ask for feedback, seek to add value, and don't forget that each interaction is an opportunity to develop a relationship that will shape your personal brand. Think long term about those touch points, especially with the people financing the industry you want to be a part of.

The Cannabis investment community is small. If you spend the timetraveling to various Cannabis investment conferences around the world like I have, you will quickly notice a lot of the same faces over and over. These people will often co-invest on deals, get each other's opinions on opportunities, or just hang out as friends.

It should be obvious to be a good, decent human and not try to dupe or take advantage of anyone. But, in case it's not, know that one act of unprofessionalism or some kind of bad behavior can lead you to be alienated really quickly. Don't mistreat anyone, whether they're an investor, intern, or anyone in between. It's simply bad for business.

Attracting Investors

My interviews revealed that personal relationship dynamics between investors and entrepreneurs are one of the biggest factors in determining whether or not a deal gets done.

Let's dive into the relationship piece of the fundraising equation.

> "You can never do enough diligence on a deal or on a group. It's very important to really understand, whether it's a partnership or whether it's a deal you're investing in, whether you're an entrepreneur bringing in a partner on the capital side: it's very important to make sure that not only is it a good business that you're investing in, but also that the people you are investing in are individuals that you would sit down for a baseball game with, go out for dinner with, and enjoy your time together. This isn't all about making money. You want to be in this with good people, you want to support good people, and there's plenty of good people to support within this industry."
>
> —David Hess,

President & Co-Founder, Tress Capital

> "When I'm looking for a partner, somebody to work with, this sounds crazy, but it's got to be somebody that I have chemistry with. It's got to be somebody that I'm friendly with, that I don't mind hanging out with, eating dinner, taking a trip with. Maybe I'm a little bit extreme with that, because I've actually started businesses with my wife. I like being friends and having a chemical bond [with people I work with]. The reason is, no matter how friendly or compatible you are, there's going to be times when there are disagreements or conflict. I like when there's an underlying friendship so that you can feel comfortable [together] and discuss tough subjects."

—Alain Bankier,
Founding Partner, New York Angels
Executive Chairman, Nexien BioPharma, Inc.

I was surprised by how frequently investors and entrepreneurs both compared the investment & fundraising process to dating. Simultaneously, both parties are courting each other, getting to know each other, and most importantly assessing the fit for a productive, successful, long term relationship. One investor even joked that it's like a business marriage.

Speaking of dating, one sunny summer afternoon in NYC, Asher Troppe, the CEO of Tress Capital, and I spontaneously went on a date together. Not like that. We were having a meeting that ran over, which may or may not have had something to do with Cannabis consumption, and were both late to meet our respective dates. For my date, I had planned for us to visit my friend's art gallery. Asher was meeting his date for a drink on the

Lower East Side. I suggested that he invite his date to the art gallery which was also in the LES. I assured him that it'd be an entertaining scene, and beyond that, my artist friend always had exotic buds. Seeing the merit in my thinking, Asher agreed to invite his date to the art gallery.

We walked over to the gallery together, continuing our spirited discussion about the future of the Cannabis industry. At the gallery, we met each other's dates, introduced them to the artist, who is a very entertaining guy, and I enjoyed some more Cannabis. As far as I could tell, a merry time was had by all. These are the kind of regular, human moments in which relationships get built. Now I know, whenever I need an investor's opinion on a deal, venture, or potential client, I can turn to Asher and count on his two cents.

Fundamentally, investors are looking for entrepreneurs who will protect and grow their capital. Entrepreneurs, at least the smart ones, are looking for investors who will add value beyond financial investment, through network, knowledge, and coaching. Ultimately, a good match is one that gives the business the greatest chance to succeed. A great match, however, can turn into huge fortunes, future ventures together, lifelong friendships, and more.

An important requirement for (business) dating success is to know what you're looking for. Are you looking to get married? Are you open to polyamory?[57] Or are you just looking for some quick action?[58] In my opinion, being direct and transparent in any

---

[57] Are you ok with an investor who has or wants to invest in your competitors?
[58] Perhaps a short term loan makes more sense for you than an equity deal?

kind of courtship interaction makes the most sense.

What is the other party looking for? Note that many investors, especially those who work at family offices, wealth management firms, or at private investment funds have investment mandates, or literal due diligence checklists of requirements for what they will and won't invest in. For example, some investors only do equity deals, some only do seed rounds, some only do ancillary business, etc.

Don't waste your precious time or anyone else's by trying to solicit someone who isn't interested in your type. Don't pitch an ancillary fund to invest in your grow op. Instead, ask them if they can introduce you to other investors who invest in grows. Offer to send them interesting ancillary businesses that might fit their deal parameters. Even if you don't know any, you will at least extend a professional courtesy and demonstrate thoughtfulness.

Lasting, successful relationships—in romance and in business—are built on trust. As an entrepreneur seeking capital investment, you're asking for another human to trust you with hundreds of thousands or even millions of dollars of their money, or money they're responsible for protecting. Appreciate how big of an ask that is. Remember, investors are human beings who deeply value their time, and thus they want to spend their work time with people they can relate to and enjoy spending time with.

The best way to earn trust is to consistently communicate clearly and act with integrity, while demonstrating a commitment to accountability and transparency. Be honest, be respectful, be kind, and be professional.

Don't fall into the trap of trying to impress, playing games, or making a bigger deal of things than they are. I've seen too many entrepreneurs react to fundraising like an insecure teenager looking for a prom date, wondering, "Why won't he respond to my emails? Did I say something stupid? I knew I shouldn't have taken that dab, he probably thinks I'm a lightweight weirdo."

Being desperate or dishonest is never attractive and it rarely works in the long term.

At this point, you might be wondering, just how difficult or competitive is it to raise private capital for a Cannabis business?

> "In 2018, there's an endless amount of investment opportunities in Cannabis, tons and tons and tons. The people who are selecting investments from all that flow, really have a choice to pick the best 10 out of a hundred, 5 out of a hundred, 1 out of a hundred. Or even to skip the entire hundred and look at the next hundred, because there's so much flow. So you really have to be buttoned up to access capital in a market where there is a lot of flow, a lot of noise, and historically a scarcity of capital."
>
> —Asher Troppe,
> CEO & Co-Founder, Tress Capital

Great Investors are Rare

The investors I interviewed for this book are bonafide professionals who focus on Cannabis and have been raising and placing money in the industry for years.

For example, Emily Paxhia, Co-Founder and Managing Director

of Poseidon Asset Management, has vetted thousands of deals, raised over a $100 million dollars for Poseidon Fund One, and has invested capital into over 100 Cannabis businesses. Aside from being bright and highly productive, Emily is a kind, pleasant, and patient human being. When she was a judge for my High Tech Hackathon, the first Cannabis software hackathon in Silicon Valley, she showed up with her adorable pup and offered each team astute feedback in a constructive, gentle way. She's the type of investor you want, one who adds value way beyond the money she brings.

Emily is an investor who is known and respected by industry insiders. Therefore, having Poseidon on your cap table signals to other investors that your business is legit and vetted, which makes attracting co-investors less painfully difficult. Naturally, over the years Emily (and her brother Morgan, also Co-Founder of Poseidon) has developed expertise and a deep network within the Cannabis industry.

Beyond that, Emily is compassionate, forgiving, and flexible. Perhaps that's due to her experience as a student and teacher of Yoga. When I first interviewed Emily for this book, I made a massive, idiotic mistake. I neglected to hit the record button at the start of our interview. After taking 30 minutes of Emily's time and concluding our interview, I realized my blunder and immediately confessed it to her. I was super embarrassed and was certain that Emily would forever think I was an idiot. Instead, she was totally understanding, non-judgemental, and generously offered me another 30 minutes of her time and a second chance to interview her.

I'm sure I was not the first (or last) entrepreneur (or human) who had screwed up in working with Emily. Her response demonstrated the quality of her character. I could easily imagine another investor telling me to "hit the road, Jack" after wasting 30 minutes of her time. Without thinking twice, Emily gave me a second chance, and also assured me that I shouldn't beat myself up over the blunder. I don't know about you, but that's the kind of investor I'd want behind me and would be motivated to perform for.

Unfortunately, the Emily Paxhia's of the world are few and far between. Indeed, Emily represents the ideal investor: competent, connected, compassionate, cool, and well capitalized. The folks you need to beware of are those who are not like Emily—and there are many of them.

Beware of Risky Investors

Not all investors are created equally. Commonly investors are categorized by the size, stage, or type of the deals they invest in.[59] Likely, you will be looking towards private equity, venture capital, hedge funds, family office investors or direct lenders to fund your Cannabis business. Rather than covering those basics here, I want to direct your attention to the fact that not all investors are assets; in fact, some can be major liabilities.

Don't be seduced by an investor just because they have—or

---

[59] Some example below, note this is not an exhaustive list:
Size: Retail, Accredited, Institutional
Stage: Seed, Series A, pre vs post revenue, growth
Type: Equity vs Debt, Passive vs Active

claim to have—money. Don't be excited by an investor just because they say they want to invest in Cannabis businesses. And definitely don't take an investor's money unless you know where it came from and what kind of human they are. This is especially true in Cannabis. It's not always easy to diligence or research an investor, but it's always necessary. Don't end up getting scammed by someone who is promising the sun and the moon, and who throws a complex contract at you that you don't understand. The easiest way to mitigate this issue is to work with an experienced Cannabis attorney.

In my early days on the Cannabis conference circuit, there was an old man who always came to events in a bowtie, fedora, and suspenders. His costume made him immediately recognizable and, like me, he spent thousands of dollars traveling the country, attending the prominent Cannabis conferences, and networking. He represented himself as a private investor and claimed to have made his money in Russia after the collapse of the Soviet Union.

As a Soviet-born person, I was immediately intrigued and suspicious of this guy given that I knew that people who did business in Russia during that time must've been very opportunistic and potentially dangerous. Post-Soviet Russia, like emerging Cannabis, was the Wild West. There were no rules, and in that environment, it is usually guerillas, gangsters, scammers, and cowboys who profit.

This man, a member of the ArcView investor network, represented himself as a friendly, polite, elderly gentleman. He regularly attended my High NY events, and yet I always got the vibe from him that he was a hustler. Not that there's anything wrong with that. I never did any business with him, other than selling him event tickets, and I was okay with that.

One day, a story hit the Cannabis media that this man had previously been convicted of fraud and larceny. He had formed political action committees to fundraise for competing presidential candidates. And according to the judge in the case, he funneled money to his for-profit consulting firm under false pretenses. A hustler indeed.

Would you want to take this guy's money? Would you trust him enough to enter into a legal business partnership together? Would you want to be associated with someone with his checkered past? I'm not sure what message his name on your cap table would send to other investors. He's the type of risky investor you want to be aware of because they might end up taking you for a ride, costing you money, and maybe even getting you jail time.

Once, at a Cannabis conference in California, I met a group of South American businessmen. Everything about their behavior indicated that they had money. We enjoyed several pre-rolls together on the deluxe party bus from the conference to a beautiful grow facility which we toured. The man who seemed to be the jefe of the crew took a liking to me. He said my big stoned smile made him happy. He said he'd never seen someone look as happy as me to be high. After more laughter and rapport building, he eventually whispered to me, "Mike I like you, if you ever need money, drugs, or women let me know." Playing along, I jokingly told him, "I always need those things."

Sensing the opportunity for a good story, I asked him how he can help me. He went on to share that his family was a successful operator in several illicit enterprises. Perhaps this explained the very intimidating man in an all black with him who had what I can only describe as resting-prison-stare face. These are not the types of guys I'd want to take money from. I imagine they are much less forgiving and compassionate than Emily Paxhia when it comes to mistakes.

A different type of risky investor to be aware of is the Cannabis newbie. In general, amateur (aka non-professional) investors are not ideal for a serious Cannabis business, beyond a friends-and-family or seed round. The Cannabis newbie is someone who has never invested in Cannabis and doesn't know much about the plant. Often, these are people without any experience in the industry. They lack realistic expectations and are likely to be tire-kickers. They'll require a lot of education and investment of your time to get them comfortable with the risks and nuances of the industry and your business.

Many of these Cannabis newbies are operating from a place of FOMO[60] and have been seduced by the hype of Cannabis or the desire to sound cool at cocktail parties by saying they've invested in a Cannabis business. The biggest problem with these investors is that they will eat up a bunch of your time, but at the end of the day they'll be unlikely to cut the check. Once they understand the risks and many hoops required for Cannabis investors to jump through, and the additional legal work and diligence required (read: money they have to spend), they will likely decide to stick to the asset classes and industries they already know. Besides,

---

[60]Fear of Missing Out

now they'll be able to talk about looking at Cannabis deals at cocktail parties and not finding the right opportunity yet. If you can, I encourage you to work with investors who have already placed money in the industry and are committed to the industry long term. They won't be as big a headache to deal with as the newbies. And they're more likely to be capable of adding value.

Note that not all Cannabis newbies make for risky investors. If they have expertise and connections in an industry that is relevant for your business, they can be huge assets. For example, if you're launching a CBD-wellness products company and your investor made their fortune in the supplements world, they can be a smart-money investor with connections to the wholesalers and distributors that will make your business thrive. Don't write someone off just because they have yet to invest in Cannabis. Instead, be aware of whether or not they've put money to work in Cannabis so you can have appropriate expectations about how much education and time they'll need before cutting a check. To find out, simply ask an investor, "What kind of Cannabis investments have you made already?" If they respond that they've only invested in Cannabis stocks, ask them if they're accredited and whether or not they've considered private placements. If not, they likely aren't going to provide meaningful financial resources.

Investing in Cannabis Stocks

People constantly ask me what Cannabis stocks to invest in and I often tell them, "That depends, how much money do you want to lose and how quickly do you want to lose it?" I say this because Cannabis stocks are broadly volatile and overpriced. Which isn't to say you can't make good money trading Cannabis stocks. I know several people who have made fortunes doing just that. But those people were hyper focused on Cannabis and put intense effort into being well informed and performing due diligence. They had much more information than the average retail investor.

Years ago, when I wrote my first book, the question of investing in public Cannabis equities was borderline absurd. There were fewer than 200 publicly traded Cannabis stocks at the time. Less than 10 actually had real businesses underlying them that were generating any revenue. Profit was a pipe dream. Was it possible to make money on those stocks? Sure. Would I recommend that investment to anyone who wasn't proficient in day trading and speculating? No.

Publicly traded Cannabis companies have evolved. There are now hundreds of investable stocks, and at least dozens with legit businesses. As a disclaimer, I'm far from the authority on stock trading, Cannabis or otherwise. And so I rarely make picks or recommend companies unless I strongly believe that a company is misvalued in the market. Speaking of which, almost every Cannabis company is misvalued in the public markets. Anyone with any knowledge of the history of financial markets can see that Cannabis stocks are in a bubble. The valuations for many of the world's largest publicly traded Cannabis companies are sky-high, some of them have traded at multiples of 100X sales and even 200X. Most of these companies gained market cap through acquisitions and top-line growth, while losing more and more money.

The business fundamentals simply don't justify the prices.

Remember the golden rule: buy low, sell high. Due to the regulatory uncertainty, downward price pressure on Cannabis products, increasing competition, and ridiculously high prices, my judgement is that most Cannabis stocks are not a good long-term buy. That being said, there are companies that have delivered solid double and even triple-digit returns in the short term. That's just not reliably accessible for the layman or retail mom-and-pop investor. Unless you're willing to be a Cannabis equity analyst and stock-picking scalper, don't bet the retirement fund on pot stocks just yet.

Cannabis Investment Risk

Cannabis is chock full of risk—every type you can think of—especially legal risk. Despite access to public and private capital markets opening up, the fact remains that Cannabis commerce is still federally illegal in the U.S. Thus, as an investor in a plant-touching business, no matter how cleverly structured your terms are, there is almost definitely going to be some paper trail that opens you up to liability in the form of criminal offenses. That means there is a potential for criminal charges including, but not limited to: drug trafficking, money laundering, wire fraud, conspiracy, continuing criminal enterprise (kingpin), and more.

I spoke about risky investors. To be fair, I must also caution prospective investors about being bamboozled by hustlers, fraudsters, and enterprising criminals. You can never do enough diligence in Cannabis!

"The industry is very small. People and companies have reputations. Connect with someone who's been in the industry for a while and leverage their network to figure out if [the person pitching you] is who they say they are, do what they say they do, and who they've worked with."

—Salmeron Barnes,[61]
Director of Growth and Strategy, Marijuana Policy Group

Aside from requesting references and checking on somebody's reputation in the industry community, it may be prudent to run a background check before you come close to cutting a check.

Don't forget about the monster that is asset forfeiture.

As recently as 2019, even without being charged with a criminal offense, Cannabis businesses, their proprietors, and even their patrons have been victims of asset forfeiture. Having your assets seized is nothing short of a catastrophe. Imagine your property being taken and then facing the financial, legal, and emotional burden of having to prove your innocence to recover your property.

"Every day you go to work you're committing an act of civil disobedience. Every one of those licensed operators is breaking a Federal law. You can risk a mandatory minimum sentence. That's a real risk, it can happen."

—Kris Krane,
Co-Founder and President, 4Front Ventures

Not that you're planning on going bankrupt, but know that Cannabis businesses are not eligible for any federal bankruptcy protections. I'm not sharing this to scare you, but rather to remind you to be extra diligent and work with attorneys,

---

[61]Marijuana Policy Group does consulting for private and public entities in Cannabis, including Canada and Colorado's regulatory bodies.

accountants, and advisors with impeccable track records and high integrity, and be prepared for what you're getting yourself into.

A final thought on Cannabis investment is that the same 5 common mistakes that Cannabis entrepreneurs make apply to Cannabis investors too. Do your research and if you can't afford to lose the money, then don't invest it in Cannabis.

Perhaps even more challenging than securing financing for your business will be finding the right human capital. Read on to the next chapter to learn about the importance of talent, teamwork, and community in building a successful Cannabis business.

13.
The Entourage Effect

"One of the things that I learned early on is this really is a relationship-based industry."

—Giadha Aguirre De Carcer,
Founder & CEO, New Frontier Data

Cannabis is the Original Social Network

The plant has a unique ability to turn strangers into fast friends. It unites people. Do not underestimate this social aspect. Embrace and appreciate it if you want to succeed in this industry.

Business is a team sport. The quality of people you have relationships with and the quality of those relationships is going to be a significant—if not *the most significant*—determinant of your success. Given the vastness of Cannabis and the variety of personalities and backgrounds it attracts, it's especially important to be critical of whom you do business with. Relationships are everything. Business doesn't grow in isolation. Teamwork is absolutely necessary to execute anything effectively at scale.

The best growers, processors, retailers, researchers, and investors don't do it alone. By the way, do you know the best growers? The retailers? The elected officials? The investors? Or, better yet, do they know you? How are you going to get their attention, trust and partnership?

Back in the day, before Cannabis commerce was rapidly being "legalized" and regulated by government bodies, it was illegal.

Today, in many parts of the world, people still go to jail and can even be sentenced to death for selling Cannabis.

Therefore, if you consider the corporate culture of the legacy Cannabis industry, you can easily understand why having a strong network and reputation would be necessary for achieving success. Given the life-or-death risks involved, working with reliable, trustworthy partners was of paramount importance for these pioneers.

Just like the Cannabis plant and all of its glorious terpenes, flavonoids, and cannabinoids, humans work more effectively in harmony than in isolation.[62] Any business achievement requires intelligent orchestration of human capital.

Today, network and reputation are still two of the most important determinants of business success, in Cannabis and every other industry.

Trust is at the core of human relationships. Your abilities, or lack thereof, to communicate clearly with sincerity, act with integrity, and offer value consistently will determine the strength of your relationships and, by extension, the strength of your personal brand. Not social media posts, marketing campaigns, or a cool logo. Although those are part of your branding, your actual personal (and professional) brand is determined by the quality of your product, performance, and impact on others.

Over the past 6 years that I've worked in the Cannabis

---

[62]The Entourage Effect refers to the synergistic interaction of various Cannabis compounds that together create a more powerful effect than when those various compounds are used in isolation.

movement, one of the things I'm most proud of is the network, relationships, and community that I have cultivated.

And I'm always happy to share my network with anyone who can truly add value to it. I welcome it. I love giving out assists.

I've had the pleasure and privilege to work with, and build friendships with, some of the most talented and dedicated leaders in Cannabis. Beyond that, I've provided thousands of New Yorkers with Cannabis education, experiences, and connections they otherwise wouldn't have received.

And that's no accident. I didn't just get high one day and all of the above magically happened. I got high a lot of days and made it happen with a lot of hard work!

The upshot is if I can go from a complete outsider, a clueless consumer, to having a vast, powerful network or entourage of Cannabis champions, you can too. And I'm about to tell you exactly how I did it—aren't you glad to have me as your Cannabis business coach?

> "Becoming really strong in your connections and connecting yourself to the best people and best professionals in this industry [is key]. You are who you surround yourself with, so if you want to be the best, if you want to be inspired by the best, then surround yourself with the best."
>
> —Chloe Villano,
> President & Founder, Clover Leaf University

Before I even met Chloe, I was aware that I am very much influenced by my environment and the people I surround myself with. In the words of legendary Life & business Coach Jim Rohn, "You are the average of the five people you spend the most time with." So I made it a point to surround myself with the greatest leaders in Cannabis in order to become one of them myself.

I'm going to take this opportunity to embarrass myself by sharing the story of meeting Chloe Villano. It was in June 2015 at the Cannabis World Congress and Business Expo (CWCBE) in NYC. This was the first time the CWCBE was being hosted at the Javits Center, one of New York's largest and most prominent convention centers, so it was a big deal for the NY Cannabis community. My business, High NY, was a promotional partner for the conference, and as part of the deal, we had a booth at the trade show. Now, mind you, this was in 2015, when High NY was very lean and mean and I was somewhat of a young punk. I figured there was no sense in spending money on an elaborate booth, swag items to give away, or any of the usual trade show marketing materials.

Instead, I showed up to the conference with some High NY'ers and we spent most of the trade show hanging out in the booth, eating edibles, and just having fun. Our booth had literally no decorations, not even a table cloth or a sign. Just the bare minimum that the conference center provided. And yet, my booth stood out significantly as one of the most popular, crowded booths at the show that year. It stood out because it was the only undecorated booth, and ironically this minimalism attracted people to come ask, "What is High NY?" which is exactly what I wanted. Secondly, the booth was full of Life.

Hundreds of people who attended the conference were members

of my community, so they were just stopping by to say, "Hi Mike Z!" and hang out. It was a grand old time.

Across from my booth and a few booths down from me, I noticed a pretty lady with a beaming smile. Filled with edibles and irrational confidence, I thought to myself I'm going to go over and charm this beautiful lady. Foolishly, I thought she was a "booth babe," hired to stand there and look pretty. And so I walked over, politely introduced myself, and asked her to tell me about the booth she was working at, Clover Leaf University.

I quickly learned that I couldn't have been more wrong in assessing the situation. This lady was no booth babe, she was Chloe Villano, the Founder and President of Clover Leaf University, the only Cannabis education program approved, regulated, and licensed by the state of Colorado's Department of Higher Education. Looking back at it, I'm ashamed to admit that my foolish misjudgments almost led me to mansplain Cannabis to her. Told you I was a young punk.

Luckily, I was able to shut up, listen, and learn. This is such a diverse and fascinating industry: the most experienced people in it are not old, white guys in suits. I asked Chloe about the educational workshop she produced for hundreds of conference attendees earlier in the day and thanked her for her leadership.

I've since learned that Chloe is an industry veteran who has just about done it all and educated masses of people along the way.

The following 4/20, I went to celebrate in Denver and took a few classes at Clover Leaf University where, thanks to Chloe, I met and learned from two Cannabis living legends, Ed Rosenthal and Adam Dunn, both Clover Leaf faculty members. One thing I admire about Chloe is that she talks and hustles like a real New Yorker, even though she's not from NYC. She's fearless, always working, and is a straight shooter who doesn't shy away from crass humor. Fun fact: Choe and I have the same birthday. Chloe, I hope you get a laugh out of this story. I've always been too embarrassed to share it with you in person.

> "One of the most worthwhile investments I have made is the time and energy spent on attending any and every meetup or seminar related to Cannabis. This allowed me to surround myself with leaders in the industry as well as aspiring entrepreneurs. I was given the chance to meet and talk to people participating in every facet of the industry from plant touching, to ancillary businesses, and Hemp. Shout out High NY circa 2014."
>
> —Steven Phan,
> Co-Founder, Come Back Daily

Cultivating Community

When I had no Cannabis network and very little Cannabis knowledge, I made it my top priority to acquire both. I was also authentically interested in bringing Cannabis education and awareness to others like me in New York. I wanted to spark the passion for Cannabis advocacy for other friends of the flower. And so I became a very committed, curious, and humble student of Cannabis.

I began reading Cannabis books. I began attending Cannabis events all over the country and asking tons of questions. I would get people's cards and email them asking for 5 – 10 minutes of their time to teach me about their area of Cannabis expertise. I also began producing High NY events, getting Cannabis students together, and offering an audience to the Cannabis experts who previously never had one in New York. Fortunately, these Cannabis leaders were eager and excited to share their knowledge with passionate humans who were hungry to learn about the plant.

My intention was to create Cannabis leaders and to build a Cannabis community. I became obsessed with those tasks. And I didn't care about making money or exploiting the plant since I was earning my living as a life and business coach. I just wanted to be of service to and advocate on behalf of the plant. I did it with a huge, genuine smile on my face.

At the time, nobody else was doing that kind of work in New York City. And few people were willing to publicly advocate and risk their reputation to be known as "The Cannabis guy." Fortunately, I had no such fear as I was committed to being a Cannabis ambassador and evangelist.

One of my favorite teachers and role models, the super coach Tony Robbins, said: "The only way to become wealthy, and stay wealthy, is to find a way to do more for others than anyone else is doing in an area that people really value." I really took that to heart, and my focus with everyone I met in the first few years of my Cannabis career was to figure out how I can help them win. And I did it, often without asking for anything in return. I just gave a lot of value because I believed that we all share success. I didn't try to make money or grow a business, I just wanted to do the right thing and make a difference. One of my mentors, a real

OG, said I was "almost pathologically helpful." Apparently, that was rare and special enough to make me stand out.

That's how I earned my reputation and developed relationships with the leaders and elders of the Cannabis community. You can do the same, just by starting locally with whatever Cannabis justice or Cannabis service organizations are in your area. And if there isn't one, start one, like I did. If you don't know how, reach out to me and I will help you. If you live in a place where that's dangerous to do, please don't put your safety at risk. Yet, if you are called to and willing to sacrifice your health or safety to fight for the plant, then bless you and I'm here to support you however I can.

My network and the trust and respect I've earned from those in it is the foundation of my success in Cannabis business. These people inspire me and also consistently bring me profitable opportunities that allow me to use my creative juices and highest thinking to make a positive impact in the community.

Bad Press Is Not Fake News

People say there's no such thing as bad press. I strongly disagree. It's not enough just to be known. You must be known for something specific and positive. A bad rep doesn't exactly inspire trust. Nor does it create lasting relationships. And it certainly doesn't facilitate business development.

Alison Ettel, former CEO of Treatwell, a well-known Cannabis-for-pets company, became a viral internet sensation in 2018 for all the worst reasons. Alison, a white lady, called the cops on an 8-year-old black girl for selling water bottles on a San

Francisco sidewalk without a permit. This incident was caught on a cell phone camera and went viral. The internet dubbed Ettel as #PermitPatty. Her actions—rightfully so—came under major scrutiny. You would figure an entrepreneur would want to support a young business woman and nurture that entrepreneurial spirit. However, that was not the case here.

Within hours, Treatwell's retailers began dropping the product, and within days Ettel resigned as CEO of the company. This story was covered by CNN, ABC, CBS, The Guardian, People, and more. Videos featuring Ettel calling the police received hundreds of thousands of views. She received lots of public shaming, some death threats, and, surely, she regrets her actions. I can't imagine it will be easy for her to work in the industry again, without, at the very least, legally changing her name.

It's hard to conceive of any good reason for Ettel's behavior. I don't know her. Perhaps she was a really wonderful and capable Cannabis business executive. However, that's now irrelevant because to the millions of people who know her through the internet, she'll always be the angry white lady who called the cops on a little black girl for no good reason. Would you want to have Permit Patty on your team? Would you give her a job at your Cannabis business? I wouldn't.[63]

Deal Breakers

I asked every single person interviewed for this book what are their biggest deal breakers when it comes to investment, hiring,

---

[63]Although I do want to give Ettel compassion and the benefit of the doubt that she's not a bad person. Hopefully she can heal and recover from this incident and move forward as a stronger person for it.

partnerships, etc.

"When I saw this question I thought, that's going to be a long list."

—Chloe Villano,
President & Founder, Clover Leaf University

"If people don't want to understand or follow the laws, that's a deal breaker for us."

—Brian Vicente,
Founding Partner, Vicente Sederberg LLC

"Lack of preparedness, dishonesty, inauthenticity. Trying too hard to pitch something. Lack of awareness that things don't always go right and lack of a plan to deal with those variable outcomes and the lack of humility to say, 'I don't know the future.'"

—Asher Troppe,
CEO & Co-Founder, Tress Capital

"There's enough clients and money to go around that I don't want to spend my limited time working directly with folks who aren't in line with me on basic values and principles."

—Kayvan Khalatbari,
Founding Partner, Denver Relief, Denver Relief Consulting,
Board of Directors, Minority Cannabis Business Association

"Somebody who's just all about the money."

—Holly Alberti,
Founder, Healthy Headie Lifestyle
Director of Marketing, iAnthus

"Because [Cannabis] is an intoxicant and illegal it brings

in many people who lack values. Going through the vetting process of every single person you deal with from public official to the person you buy your stickers from, it's very time consuming."

—Christie Lunsford,
CEO, The Hemp Biz Conference

"Make sure you do a good job of vetting out who you're working with...because it's a very good way to get burned."

—Jim McAlpine,
President, Aura Ventures

Kris Krane, Mowgli Holmes, Christian Hageseth, and others offered a simple deal breaker that I firmly agree with. They elegantly called it the "No Assholes Rule."[64]

Remember, most people who are leading this industry and who are deeply committed to Cannabis innovation are doing it because they believe in a higher purpose than financial gain. Most, if not all, of those people have made significant sacrifices to be in this industry and come from a background of Cannabis activism.

Thus, they're not willing to make exceptions for so-called assholes, or those who do not embody compassion, kindness, integrity, and loyalty to the cause and for the greater mission of Cannabis empowerment. As in any other industry, the most successful people have the luxury of being very selective about with whom they choose to work. Like Kayvan said, why bother

---

[64]Mowgli has become a controversial figure since I first met him. Google it if you like. Ironically, some of his original customers now think he's an asshole.

wasting precious time with someone who isn't aligned with your core values and principles? What's the fun in that?

Once upon a time, early in my Cannabis business career, I worked with an asshole. He was smart, well connected, and had what I (at the time) considered to be an impressive background in business. So I was willing to overlook the fact that his values were not aligned with mine in terms of prioritizing Cannabis justice over capital gains. In fact, I even believed that it was good that he was so ruthlessly focused on money and that we'd balance each other out. Unfortunately, I learned the hard way that working with an asshole is a great way to end up in a shitty situation.

When I tried to sever our working relationship, this person became extremely vindictive and obsessed with hurting me. Not only did he try to steal my business assets, but he also tried to destroy my personal and professional reputation by shamelessly defaming me every chance he got, reaching out to my partners, customers, and even personal friends to slander me, until a judge ordered him to stop.

Ultimately, this person only succeeded in tarnishing his own reputation. I learned an important lesson in that experience, which is that no amount of capital, competence, or charisma can make up for a lack of character.

Keep that in mind when you're evaluating prospective entrepreneurs, investors, partners, employees, employers, spouses, friends, and mentors.

Diversity & Inclusion

I'm going to keep this short, sweet, and to the point. Diversity is one of nature's greatest assets. If you don't embrace and seek diversity on your team, you're missing out on a huge competitive advantage.

Cannabis leaders have long known what other members of the business community are just now waking up to: having a diverse management team and workforce leads to improved performance. Multiple studies have now shown that diverse teams and companies do better than their less diverse competitors.[65]

> "I've been very fortunate that we were able to build a team that's extremely diverse. When you look at our crew, we have everything, age-wise, ethnicity-wise, sexual orientation-wise, religion-wise, political affiliation-wise, and it really has allowed us to have as few blind spots as possible because we have a truly diverse group of folks that have very different ways of thinking and looking at things."
>
> —Giadha Aguirre De Carcer,
> Founder & CEO, New Frontier Data

The nature of Cannabis is inclusive and non-discriminatory. Cannabis crosses all cultural divides and has no concern for the constructs of race, religion, sexual orientation, and other differences that humans tend to dwell on.

---

[65] https://www.mckinsey.com/business-functions/organization/our-insights/why-diversity-matters - just one example

Cannabis leaders are generally tolerant, friendly, and, therefore, value inclusivity. We look for similarities and points of connection, rather than differences to separate us. So, if you don't, you might run into issues.

> "This industry is very open and tolerant. We actually tolerate people who don't smoke pot. You never hear people make fun of someone who doesn't [consume Cannabis]. That's not considered cool."
>
> —Mowgli Holmes
> Co-Founder & CEO, Phylos Bioscience

Also, Cannabis business people are generally aware of and sensitive to the racially problematic history of Prohibition.[66] If not, they need to be educated.

That being said, I recognize that as a white male, I'm privileged to be in this industry and my experience is going to be very different from that of a woman of color. I recognize my responsibility to share or use my privilege to bring others up and empower them.

I also acknowledge that I can't try to rescue people and act like "the great white hope." Rather than trying to address it myself, I asked the Cannabis leaders of color whom I interviewed if they had any advice specifically for BIPOC Cannabis professionals and entrepreneurs.

---

[66]And to the racial challenges still very much present in society and Cannabis today. Especially in terms of creating economic equity for communities that were disproportionately harmed by the War on Drugs.

Advice from BIPOC Cannabis Entrepreneurs for BIPOC

"Don't be scared. A lot of POC are very afraid of Cannabis because of the laws surrounding it, because those laws were designed to keep us down. I understand all the PTSD around Cannabis in communities of color. I want to encourage people of color, don't be scared, we've got to move forward full speed ahead. You have to be very street smart... get some people who look like you, get together and figure out a plan."

—Amber Senter,
CEO, Leisure Life Products
Co-Founder & Executive Director, Supernova Women

"Network with other entrepreneurs of color. I am a resource for anybody who's reading this interview, contact me: Shanel@ArdentCannabis.com. We have resources for you. There's a Minority Cannabis Business Association, get involved with these groups. One thing that entrepreneurs of color sometimes don't have access to is a network. You have to be very, very intentional about building a network of entrepreneurs, building up a network of people that are related to money, potential investors, continuing and developing those relationships and being very intentional about that. And also about seeking out mentors and seeking out mentors of different races and genders because those people are going to be champions for you, because, trust me, when they see you and they've seen how hard you work and what you can produce, they're going to be very impressed, and they will help you navigate and get different opportunities. Networking and mentorship are definitely key. Please do reach out, because we are here for you, so that's the first step."

—Shanel Lindsay,
Founder & President, Ardent Cannabis
Member of the Massachusetts Cannabis Advisory Board

"Build your network of allies. Whether that's attending High NY events or attending a Women Grow event, or attending a festival networking event, try and get out there and build a community around you of people that will validate your ideas and people that will act as references. Those allies should be as diverse as the community you want to see around you. Don't just go to people in the Cannabis industry. Also find business leaders in your local community that believe in you and understand what you're trying to do, because ultimately that helps strengthen our industry when we can bring in unlikely allies."

—Caroline Phillips,
Founder, National Cannabis Festival

"We are truly walking in historic times because we are the only ones who will experience the end of prohibition of Cannabis and can do something about it. Your success will be the blueprint for someone you haven't met yet, so be aware of how closely you're being watched."

—Leo Bridgewater,
National Director of Veterans Outreach,
Minorities 4 Medical Marijuana

"For my Latinx community, the most important advice I

can give is to start the Cannabis conversation at home. Not just here in the United States, but with our families and friends back home. Education is key and if you can convince a conservative family member, there is nothing you can't accomplish in this space. This industry is coming, there is an opportunity for economic growth like we have never seen before here in the U.S. and abroad. Now is the time to invest your efforts."

—Nelson Guerrero,
Founder and Executive Director, Cannabis Cultural Association

"Follow the words of the late Nipsey Hussle: 'We don't want advances, we want equity. We don't want one-off endorsements, we want ownership.' Do not allow this space to be taken from you by using political strategy (lobbying), community activation, and ethical business approaches. Understand that this industry is built on the casualties of the racist War On Drugs that still criminalize black and brown people. Do not be swept aside as just another consumer. Be prepared to stand up for something other than money. Be ready to pace yourself and make mistakes. Do not allow yourself to be minimized or tokenized by any large entities who only view you as a pawn for bolstering their license application. Let people know you're the one in charge and not the help."

—Jacob Plowden,
Deputy Director, Cannabis Cultural Association

The Cannabis Cultural Association has a very special place in my heart. I met Jake and Nelson at their respective first Cannabis industry events. We later bonded over some bowls and Nelson approached me for feedback about doing a Latinx outreach effort for my company, High NY.

I loved the idea and told him that he identified a significant gap in the market. However, I encouraged him to pursue that through his own venture and not under mine. Why? Because leaders create leaders. Investing in the movement by developing leaders is more important to me than building my business.

Instead of inviting Nelson to work for me, I introduced him to a few people who I thought shared his vision and eventually a few of them went on to form the Cannabis Cultural Association (CCA). I've collaborated with CCA on community education events as well as fundraisers for Cannabis justice causes.

Among many other contributions to the movement, CCA sued Jeff Sessions and the Department of Justice. That's dedication. It's been amazing to witness what Nelson, Jake, and the CCA have achieved.

I am also grateful for the countless laughs we've shared together along our Cannabis journeys. If you're ever lucky enough to stand in a cypher with the three of us, bring an extra ass or some duct tape because you will be in danger of laughing your ass off. Shoutout to the whole CCA Board, you are some of the most genuine, badass, righteous people in the Cannabis community.

14.
How to Fail Correctly

"Every failure is an opportunity to learn. If you don't learn from your failures, then you deserve to fail. When I was younger, I was a boxer. In the ring, the rule is a winner is someone who gets up one more time than the number of times you're knocked down. That is it; it was very simple, you just keep getting up and that's your tenacity, that's your grit."

—Francis Priznar,
SVP and Chief Mentor, The Arcview Group

"I've had so many failures but I like to call them lessons because I haven't ever failed if I've learned something from it. A failure is when you go on a pity party, and withdraw, and say, 'I'm done.' For me, it's like, 'Okay, so that was a hard lesson. I got it. Now I don't have to do it again.'"

—Mara Gordon,
Founder, Aunt Zelda's

Fear of failure is one of the most powerful and destructive forces in the world. It's responsible for a lot of pain, regret, and human suffering.

In Cannabis business, failure is guaranteed, but suffering is optional.

The nature of entrepreneurship requires risk taking. Perfection is a myth and, thus, failure is a given. It is not something to fear, but rather something to acknowledge and learn from. It's an important part of the growth process. Often, we learn more from our failures than from our victories. Fortunately, when it comes to Cannabis business, there's no shortage of opportunities to mess things up.

Persistence, grit, and determination are all muscles you will strengthen when exercising entrepreneurship. The only way to gain experience is by taking imperfect action and learning from the outcomes. There will be many times of uncertainty when, as a leader, you will have to make a tough decision with limited information. You must understand up front that you will get things wrong. It's simply inevitable. Accept it, and when it happens be kind and compassionate to yourself.

In coaching dozens of entrepreneurs, I've noticed a dangerous pattern that looks like this:

1. Overanalyzing to try and find a perfect plan
2. An inability to execute quickly because of slowed momentum
3. Concern about the slowed momentum
4. Anxious second-guessing of the already overanalyzed plan
5. Deep frustration about the lack of positive results
6. Sadness, guilt, shame, and loss of confidence
7. Continued lack of action
8. Poor results
9. Back to step 1

Having gone through that vicious cycle more times than I'd like to admit, I can earnestly tell you that it is painful. In fact, the best way to deal with that cycle is to avoid it altogether. How? By giving yourself permission to fail and be imperfect from the start.

Thomas Edison famously joked, "I have not failed. I've just found 10,000 ways that won't work." Ultimately he persevered, created the light bulb, and had a tremendous impact on society with his innovations. Be lit like Thomas Edison.

Growth Occurs Outside the Comfort Zone

> "I could give you tons and tons of examples of failures, because I'm a risk taker. When you take risks and you're a pioneer, you fail at least as much as you succeed, and oftentimes, it seems like you fail a whole lot more."
>
> —Steve DeAngelo,
> Co-Founder, Harborside Dispensary Group

If you're not failing regularly, then chances are you're not taking enough big, bold actions. Make it a habit to regularly step beyond your comfort zone as an entrepreneur. Please note, I'm not saying to do anything crazy and then convince yourself it's for the sake of growth. Don't try to be a mule for a cartel because it's risky and puts you outside your comfort zone. Don't compromise your values—that's the wrong kind of discomfort. Instead, compromise on your insecurity, fear, or inexperience. Write a press release, even if you have never done it before. Produce a podcast, even if you're not tech savvy. Invest money in your business or education, even if it feels expensive. These types of visits outside the comfort zone produce growth.

Acknowledge and appreciate your fear.

Allow it to guide you to the edge of your comfort zone and toward opportunities for evolution. Fear is a natural animal instinct all human beings experience. The common reactions to fear are fight, flight, or freeze. I invite you to befriend and study your fear. Learn what it physically feels like in your body. When you notice it, acknowledge and welcome the fear. Then inquire about it, ask what am I afraid of here? Greet fear with curiosity and compassion. Then, make a decision about one small courageous step you can take beyond your fear. Or create a story that contradicts the one causing you to feel afraid.

As Nelson Mandela once said, "courage is not the absence of fear, but the triumph over it. The brave [person] is not [one] who does not feel afraid, but [one] who conquers that fear."

Be cautious not to let someone else's skepticism or negativity influence your thinking. Allow yourself to experiment and test new ideas even when others misunderstand or criticize you. Give yourself the time, space and permission to fail forward.

Learning from failed experiments is the essence of the scientific method and will accelerate your path to success. Anticipate failure, don't fear it.

> "Any recoverable failure is fine. Just know you have to build in time for failure in your business model."
> —Evan Nison,
> Founder & CEO, NisonCo PR

> "I fail every day and I love failing because that means I'm trying something that's unproven. And if you want to expand, you have to try what's unproven. Don't be afraid

to do that. My favorite failures are probably my biggest ones. I don't dwell on my losses, what I do is I reverse-engineer how they failed."

—Garyn Angel
CEO, Magical Butter

Cannabis entrepreneurs with the high mindset embrace failure. Sure, everyone prefers winning to losing. However, it is important to be realistic and understand that rejection, failure, and defeat are temporary states and just par for the course. In my enterprise sales days at Google, we often joked that each "no" gets us closer to a "yes."

Fail gracefully, fail spectacularly, and fail frequently. As long as you're failing forward and learning lessons along the way, you're gaining valuable experience and getting closer to success.

15.
The Dark Side of Cannabis Entrepreneurship

Being an entrepreneur can be isolating and downright painful. It's not a lifestyle that most people will really ever understand. It requires a high risk tolerance to give up the stability and structure of a 9 to 5. Don't believe the hype: entrepreneurs who are publicly praised and coveted for their glamorous lifestyles are the few and far between. In order to earn those spots, you better believe they endured a lot of challenges, struggles, pain, misery, and despair.

Working around the clock on a startup business in a highly-regulated, unpredictable, bleeding-edge industry like Cannabis will require great sacrifices and is guaranteed to test your mental fortitude. Hell, it might even push you to the limits and beyond, leaving you broken.

The highs are high and the lows are low.

Left Behind

I have a friend who was interviewed for this book, only he wasn't included in the book. He was the Co-Founder of a high-profile, Cannabis tech company. The company he created earned press coverage in every media outlet you could think of, raised millions of dollars from venture capitalists, and attracted talented executives from mainstream, internationally-known brands. My friend, a fantastic, genius human with a heart of gold left a successful career in tech to join Cannabis because he was called to help medical patients after seeing a loved one get relief from Cannabis during a battle with cancer. He is well liked in the activist community because he's a genuinely kind guy, with a great sense of humor, and he's an absolute pleasure to share a joint with.

Unfortunately, the last time I saw him, when I asked how he was doing, he told me he was broke and depressed. I laughed, believing that he was just joking in his usual sarcastic, playful way. But then I noticed that he was completely serious. I quickly apologized for my laughter and inquired about his situation. I learned that he was grieving. He was grieving the loss of his business, and, I suspect, also of his self-esteem.

He shared with me that his company's board of directors was unhappy with the rate of progress and decided to remove him from his executive role, leaving him with a minimal financial stake in the company, due to a perceived lack of performance.[67]

He was angry, sad, and deeply ashamed of his situation, especially after being paraded publicly as the company's golden boy. He felt used and manipulated by his investors. Worst of all, he felt hopeless and like he could never work in the Cannabis industry again or even show his face at an industry event. I was shocked and deeply saddened to see this beautiful human so damaged by the business that he created.

What surprised me even more was that over the next few days and weeks, he shared a lot of his struggles on social media. Given

[67]Be extra careful to the terms you agree to when accepting investment! Have you found a trustworthy Cannabis lawyer yet?

that we share many mutual friends in the industry, I was impressed by his courage and vulnerability in expressing the pain and hardship he was experiencing. I judge it wasn't easy to do. What was beautiful, however, was the response of the Cannabis community.

Several entrepreneurs offered compassion, words of encouragement, support, and new opportunities so this man could get back to work, feel better, and support his family. Eventually he got back on his feet and is again doing well in the technology industry.

Some stories don't end so well. Research from UCSF suggested that nearly one third of entrepreneurs are living with depression. There have been several suicides by highly-visible and highly-successful entrepreneurs in recent years.

Constant stress, long work hours, uncertainty, unpredictability, social isolation, and big out-of-this-world, lofty, all-or-nothing goals make for a dangerous combination. When your definition of success is very narrow and very difficult to achieve, you're setting yourself up for pain and suffering.

It's great to be ambitious; however, you must be OK taking the entrepreneur's journey, knowing that you may never succeed. Taking the journey in earnest is success. However, if your definition of success is building the world's largest Cannabis brand and becoming the wealthiest Cannabis entrepreneur of all time, then, especially if you consider all other outcomes to be failures, you're likely going to feel like a failure. That's not a good, nor healthy way to feel, certainly not for long stretches of time.

Low Mike Z

Nobody is immune to failure, and nobody is immune to the trauma, stress, and even depression that failure may cause. I learned this lesson the hard way.

A few years ago, I got roped into a frivolous litigation. If you've never been sued in Federal court, believe me when I tell you, it's no picnic. Even though I knew that the truth and justice were on my side, the situation was still psychologically and financially stressful.

For the months that I was embroiled in this legal battle, the massive amount of energy and attention required to produce documents for discovery, take phone calls with attorneys, deal with sleazebag tactics, wait for procedural turning points, and so on took a toll on me. Alternating between indignant anger and existential fear, the emotional rollercoaster left me depleted. My creativity was shot. I felt isolated, threatened, and stuck. Without even realizing it, I had fallen into a depression.

It occurred to me one weekday morning when I was alone in my apartment, lying facedown on my couch. I'd just taken another bong rip, and it failed to bring me any pleasure, nor did it numb my anxiety. I looked at the clock. It wasn't even 10 AM yet. All I could think about was how slowly time was moving, how little time had passed since I last checked the clock, and how much I wanted the day to end so I could go back to sleep.

Thankfully, that sad thought shocked me back to Life. I saw that I was avoiding living and immediately decided that I was better than that. I refused to give away my zest and vitality because of some First World problems. I tried to laugh it off, remembering the few supportive folks who told me, "You know you've made it when someone sues you." It didn't feel good, especially when the retainer needed to be replenished; watching the legal fees grow and my bank account shrink made me nauseous. But I reminded myself of one of my mentor's aphorisms, "Never worry about what can be replaced with money."

I decided to look at things on the bright side and treat the lawsuit as my ad-hoc law school education. I decided to view the challenging times to be a test in toughness and an opportunity to develop greater resilience. Before I knew it, the case was settled in my favor and I returned back to business as usual. Or so I thought.

A year after the lawsuit had settled, business had gotten back to normal. But I hadn't. Whereas in the past, I had perhaps been trusting to a fault, in my new normal, I found it incredibly difficult to trust anyone. My adversary in the lawsuit was someone who initially approached me as a mentor and claimed they had my best interests at heart. Yet, when my best interests were no longer in line with his, he showed his true colors.

I hadn't fully appreciated how disruptive the lawsuit was to my psyche. I sensed that I needed help to overcome my trust issues, which was especially tricky because I didn't trust anyone, even the people closest to me. I was paranoid that anyone who expressed concern for me was setting me up. I justified it by remembering the Notorious B.I.G.'s *10 Crack Commandments*:

"Number 3, never trust no-bo-dy
Your moms'll set that ass up, properly gassed up

> Hoodied and masked up, for that fast buck
> She'll be laying in the bushes to light ya ass up."

Unfamiliar problems require outside-the-box solutions. So for the first time in my Life, I sought the help of a therapist. As I've stated earlier in this book, I believe every adult human has experienced trauma. Therefore, I believe everyone can benefit from therapy. Even if you're not actively suffering and don't think you have any mental health problems, therapy is still a great tool for developing self awareness, resilience, empathy, and communication skills. Beyond that, it's wise to strengthen your psychological foundation when things are steady, instead of scrambling to make repairs once a crisis hits.

It's a shame that in so many cultures, there is still a stigma around therapy. Don't let other people's judgements prevent you from investing in your mental health. You deserve to raise your consciousness, attain a higher mindset, and enjoy greater well-being.

When you're working hard towards a higher purpose, don't get deluded into thinking that your business success determines your worth as a human being.

Self Worth > Net Worth

Don't ever believe that you're a loser if you don't win in business. That is the absolute wrong way to fail. Instead, even if your business doesn't succeed, honor your courage for trying. Above all, honor your obligation to your own health and self care. There's more to Life than making money.

Just by nature of being human, of being you, you're worthy of compassion, love, and connection. You don't have to earn that with Cannabis business success or any other professional achievement.

Often entrepreneurs, especially less experienced ones, are bad at creating and enforcing boundaries between themselves and their businesses. These are the same entrepreneurs who are hustling hard to build their companies and are often bootstrapped or running lean. Therefore, they often think the answer to challenges is to work harder or longer. And so they do, but at what cost?

Frequently the first thing these highly ambitious achiever types sacrifice is their own health and well-being. This looks like less sleep, eating the convenient, less nutritious fast food, skipping the gym, or missing the fun downtime with friends. Those are dangerous patterns to get into. And, yes, creating a successful business requires sacrifice, but I'd encourage you AVOID compromising on your health and safety as much as possible.

I've coached scores of entrepreneurs, Cannabis business people, and high performing professionals who were suffering from burnout. I have experienced burnout. It's not pretty. It undermines your relationships, your sense of self-worth, your creativity, and your performance. To deal with it requires rest and activities that recharge the mind, body, and spirit. Better yet is to avoid burnout altogether by pacing yourself and prioritizing self-care.

Mindful Entrepreneurship

One of my coaching outcomes that I'm most proud of is that

I've helped all of my clients build and maintain a consistent meditation practice. I've even gotten a few into yoga, too! I'm a huge fan of meditation: it's essentially stress relief, healing, and brain exercise all in one—a personal development junkie's dream! I know for a fact that every human can meditate and that every human would benefit from meditation. It's just like regular physical exercise, a healthy diet, and getting adequate sleep. Everyone knows that these habits are the building blocks of health.

Unfortunately, it's easy to know what's right and still do what's wrong. It's easy to make excuses and push things off. Similarly, all work and no play is unhealthy. We need time away from our work to recharge the creative energies. We need a healthy separation to simply enjoy being. You can't always be doing and efforting, that is not a healthy work-life balance.

Don't procrastinate on investing in and protecting your health and well-being. As the leader or executive of your Cannabis business, especially if it's in the early or start-up phases, you are often the greatest asset your business has. Your talent, time, and energy are the inputs that make the business grow. Therefore, your health is the greatest asset you have. Protecting that asset is critical to running a productive, healthy business. So when you find yourself thinking your business can benefit at the expense of your self-care and personal well-being, think again.

Finally, always know that asking for help when you need it is a sign of strength, not weakness. Don't fail yourself by not asking for support when you need it.

Stay Out of Jail

Seriously. Don't go. Not a single person I've met who's served time had anything nice to say about it.

Unless you're protesting, volunteering with inmates, or visiting someone, don't go. I can't imagine many scenarios where going to prison is good for your Cannabis business. Unless you're a criminal defense lawyer.

My humble advice is be militant about compliance and don't break the law. That's tricky because any Cannabis business in America is technically breaking Federal law.

Illegal Cannabis Business

If you're actively planning on operating illegal Cannabis enterprises, that's really beyond my scope of expertise and the only advice I can offer is don't get caught. I don't encourage anyone to get into the illicit industry. Yet, I understand why some folks are ok taking that risk.

The illicit Cannabis industry is thriving; it's full of opportunity and will likely continue to grow for the next few years. The majority of Cannabis commerce still happens illegally.

If you're already an underground operator, I understand why as an entrepreneur you'd prefer to be in an unregulated arena rather than in a highly-regulated and taxed business environment. It doesn't take much calculus to figure that out. I don't want to knock anybody's hustle.

Personally, I am sympathetic to the rationale that Cannabis never should have been illegal in the first place, and, thus, the law is not worthy of respect or adherence. I've heard it argued that illicit Cannabis operators are some of the greatest activists, especially those who risked their personal freedom supplying what Cannabis patients and consumers demanded. It's true, those entrepreneurs paved the way for Cannabis business.

Will the underground Cannabis market survive in the long term? How many alcohol bootleggers do you know? Then again, Cannabis isn't alcohol.

In any case, I believe the future of Cannabis business is legal and regulated and so I highly encourage newcomers to stick to legal green.

16.
The Grass is Always Greener

> "There's room for everyone in this space. Anybody who's doing it legally and sustainably will survive, especially if they can work together with others."
>
> —Danielle Schumacher,
> CEO, THC Staffing Group

Cannabis is Abundant

With $150 Billion of annual global demand for Cannabis, there's more than enough opportunity for you to make a very comfortable or even a lavishly, luxurious living.

Don't be greedy. Don't be an asshole. You never get higher in Life by taking others lower. And if you get pleasure out of doing so, you're an asshole.

Instead, be generous and generative. When you are in the position to lend someone else a helping hand or facilitate their growth or success, please—for the love of Ganja—do it. I'd argue it's your obligation to do so.

Remember all the times someone—a mentor, a friend, a partner, or a parent—went out of their way to help you. Remember the times you've ever received a gift of kindness, support, or Cannabis. Don't just be the recipient, take joy in giving and helping others. That's the essence of Cannabis: to give, to elevate, and to restore. Cannabis is indiscriminately generous. It doesn't matter your age, race, religion, gender or sexuality, the plant will offer you its gifts. Be like Cannabis.

Be kind and respectful to everyone, unless they prove unworthy of basic human decency, in which case they're likely suffering. Extend compassion to those in pain, those in need, and those who might not be in as high a place as you. When you do it, you'll feel good and you'll serve as a positive ambassador for the greater Cannabis community.

In case doing the right thing isn't a good enough reason for you to do the right thing, then also consider that you never know who will become the Bill Gates or Beyonce of weed. You never know the full story or power of the person you're interacting with, so default to treating everyone you meet with love and kindness.

Think again about what kind of Cannabis industry you want to co-create and participate in. What kind of world do you want to live in? What do you want the next generation to live like? Let that be your motivation. Act from a place of abundance, rather than from greed. Greed is the toxic byproduct of fear.

Community Reinvestment

Consider donating 10% of your business profits to charitable causes and to Cannabis justice organizations. This is a great way to institutionalize community reinvestment into your business. This is especially important when you become financially successful, but you don't have to wait until you're a Cannabis tycoon to give back and support those who are less fortunate than you.

10% of the profits from my NYC Cannabis Film Festival go to The Ghetto Film School, a nonprofit that provides video production training and opportunities to young people of color.

5% of my profits from this book will be donated to Students for Sensible Drug Policy (SSDP), an organization that trains college students to become drug policy advocates and engage in civics.

Another 5% will be donated to Defy Ventures, a nonprofit that provides entrepreneurship education, coaching, job training, re-entry resources, funding and much more to formerly incarcerated people. These organizations do work that I deeply appreciate. I am privileged to be able to contribute to their missions.

By purchasing this book, you're supporting SSDP and Defy, too. You're helping to empower the next generation of drug policy leaders and providing formerly incarcerated people with positive opportunities to earn an honest living. Doesn't that feel nice? See how easy it can be to invest in the community?

Create an ethos of paying it forward and inspire everyone you work with to practice the habit of charitable giving and community reinvestment. That's the kind of example Cannabis leaders must model. Plus, it will train the compassion muscle, which is a critical one for fulfillment in Life.

By the way, your contributions don't have to be financial. You can volunteer your time and expertise to people in need as well. However you give back, make sure you do it in a way that is significant and consistent.

Invest in Activism

When you're running a business, you won't have much time to lobby Congress, educate politicians, and be an activist. Fortunately, many talented, passionate, hard working people are devoting themselves to activism. Honor their commitment by volunteering with or donating to organizations, dedicated to ending Prohibition, like the ones listed below:

- Americans for Safe Access
- Cannabis Cultural Association
- Doctors for Cannabis Regulation
- Drug Policy Alliance
- Marijuana Policy Project
- Minorities for Medical Marijuana
- Minority Cannabis Business Association
- National Cannabis Industry Association
- NORML
- Patients Out of Time
- Students for Sensible Drug Policy
- SuperNova Women
- Veterans for Medical Marijuana

Cannabis business is a team sport and the bigger picture is about making the human community and the plant community more healthy and connected. If you're healthy enough to play the game, then keep in mind the patients and people who don't have those same privileges. Lift them up and don't underestimate the difference you can make for someone else and even for everyone else. You have the power to build an abundant future.

> "There's an abundance out there. Go get what's yours."
> —Garyn Angel,
> CEO, Magical Butter

17.
The Future of The Cannabis Industry

Nobody knows what's coming next in Cannabis business, so don't get distracted by disagreement over where Cannabis is going. Everyone is entitled to their own opinions, but more will be wrong than right.

There's a lot of transformation in store for Cannabis business. Politics are still a huge part of the process. Sensible taxation and banking laws are still not in place as of this writing. Adequate medical research is still not being done in the U.S.

The fight to re-legalize is far from over.

As someone who has studied Cannabis business from the inside while learning from the top experts, here are some predictions of what will emerge in Cannabis in the next few years. Keep in mind, the views expressed here are just my thoughts.

The Bifurcation of Medical & Adult-Use Cannabis

As more states and countries come on board and Cannabis is rescheduled—or ideally de-scheduled—on the Federal level, Medical Cannabis will start to resemble other pharmaceutical products. Unfortunately, this may eliminate the jobs of the healers, medicine makers, and passionate Cannabis champions that have cared for patients for many years. Scientists and researchers are still making discoveries about proper dosage, how to apply Cannabis to address specific ailments, and what cannabinoids and terpenes are responsible for which therapeutic benefits.

The requirement of precise dosage, as well as the need for consistent cannabinoid combinations and formulations, will result in the pharmaceuticalization of Cannabis. To achieve this, production methods will change from techniques of traditional plant medicine to industrial, pharmacological processes. For example, lab-grown, yeast-based cannabinoids which will allow for the scale and cost effectiveness required to make huge batches of specifically and consistently formulated Cannabis compounds.

The adult use, social, or "inspirational" market, meanwhile, will look much more like the alcohol industry. Indeed, the investment of major alcohol and tobacco brands into major Cannabis companies indicates this inevitability. Surely, these companies will mess things up for everyone. They are built on principles of exploitation and will exploit the plant with little regard for its sanctity. Since their business models are built on maximum usage, they will use marketing to encourage people to over-consume the plant. Anything to make a green buck and increase shareholder value.

Unlike big alcohol and big tobacco, I predict that "big Cannabis" will struggle to become a market-dominating force. It will take them at least a generation and some very clever marketing to gain adoption. Most Cannabis users will not trust, nor want to support, huge corporate Cannabis conglomerates if other options are available.

Instead, big corporate Cannabis will have to acquire portfolios of craft Cannabis brands and leverage the brand loyalty and trust of artisanal producers to gain a following.

Cannabis consumers don't want to line the pockets of fat cat capitalists who can simply offer cheaper, mass-produced Wal-Mart weed. Aside from the most price-sensitive buyers, most Cannabis consumers will want to purchase products grown with love and care by passionate Cannabis farmers.

Despite increased economic pressure and competition from big Cannabis, mom-and-pop craft producers and artisans will never go out of style. And if they are priced out, like many are sadly being in legal markets, then the underground will come back stronger than before.

The Emergence of Big Brands, With Edibles First

We'll have some highly corporate mega brands as well as craft-bud producers.

Marley Naturals, Leafs By Snoop, Willie's Reserve—they are trying to become the Coca-Cola of Cannabis. And so far, they're all failing. There are very few Cannabis product brands that are known en masse, by consumers and non-consumers alike. There is no Apple or McDonalds of Cannabis. This is largely due to fragmented markets and advertising restrictions. The majority, if not all, of the big Cannabis brands that most Cannabis consumers know are homegrown, a.k.a. built by people who come from the Cannabis culture and community. Yet, even they have not come close to achieving household brand name status.

Only a few edibles, concentrates, and flower brands are known by the majority of Cannabis consumers. In those 3 segments, I believe that edibles brands have the best chance of crossing over into mainstream recognition.

Concentrates are a bit too esoteric. Flowers are too difficult to scale, repeat consistently, and differentiate. Edibles, however, because of their form factor, are familiar enough to become household brand names. The same way Altria, the owner of Marlboro, and Constellation Brands, owners of Corona, are vying to capture Cannabis market share to mitigate against the declines their businesses face as Cannabis becomes more accessible, the Hershey's and Doritos of the world will also inevitably enter the Cannabis market. Thus, edibles brands will face potentially tougher competition than companies making buds or extracts.

At the end of the day, quality is king. Consistency is queen. Culture is the ace, so those who can connect with consumers and represent the culture in a good way will have the best chance at building lasting brands.

DIY Cannabis

Access to Cannabis information and product variety will only become easier for consumers. Once consumers cross the education chasm and better understand the fundamentals of the endocannabinoid system and the versatility of the plant, a significant portion of the market, especially the heaviest consumers, will begin experimenting with DIY Cannabis.

More and more people will begin cooking edibles at home, making their own tinctures and salves, and even begin growing their own plants, especially as these processes become easier with consumer technology.

Other ingestion methods are going to become more common for the average daily consumer. People will become more precise and personalized in how they use Cannabis. This is more economical and, for enthusiasts, this will open up a new avenue for engaging with the plant.

Most adult use markets have seen infused products (edibles) and concentrates take significant market share away from flower. The prevalence of smoking as an ingestion method will continue to decline; however, it will never go away completely. There will always be a traditional cultural aspect that comes with rolling something, passing it around, and putting smoke in the air. It is a sacred Cannabis ritual that will not go out of style. Or maybe it will, I don't know. Especially after Covid19, the ritual of puffing and passing is potentially at risk.

Ultimately, the convenience and discretion offered by vape pens, edibles, tinctures, and topicals will lead more consumers to turn away from combustion. After all, smoking does have adverse health effects.

Less THC & More Microdosing

As we get more scientific evidence and a deeper understanding of the Cannabis plant, THC, and CBD will become less important. Consumers and producers will emphasize terpenes, other cannabinoids, cannabinoid acids, and other elements of the plant that impact mammal organisms. High-THC products will become more strictly regulated, and some places might put limits on THC intake and potency, especially for social use.

Furthermore, my personal anecdotal research suggests that too much THC is not a good thing. Too much of anything has adverse effects on the human body. THC and CBD are no different. As consumers become more informed about their minimum effective dose and consumption becomes more personalized, micro-dosing will prevail as a more popular practice.

More Scandals

2019 saw a huge scandal around illegal vape pens. All over America, people were hospitalized with popcorn lung and other mysterious respiratory ailments, some of which resulted in death. Media outlets reported several potential causes, from thinning agents that were cut into underground Cannabis vape cartridges to heavy metal poisoning resulting from cheap vape pen hardware. While this may have been the first and only major Cannabis related health scandal in this decade to penetrate public consciousness, it certainly won't be the last as legalization advances.

Death of the Dispensary

I just don't see the Cannabis dispensary existing in a significant way in a decade or two. Likely there will be some Cannabis retail stores or boutiques, like craft wine shops or huge liquor mega stores. Especially as Cannabis legalization spreads, in an e-commerce world, I just don't see why Cannabis would have its own stores. The wholesale price of flower will continue to decline. We'll eventually be able to buy prepackaged bud and infused products in dispensaries, grocery stores, at the farmer's market, and online. Pharmacies and drug stores will sell medical

Cannabis products. They already sell CBD.

While dispensaries and Cannabis retail businesses are attractive in the short and medium term, I don't see it as a viable business in a decade or two. The exception is building a franchise and becoming the Starbucks of weed. Good luck with that!

Once federal legalization happens and big box retailers start slanging dope, dispensaries will disappear like mom-and-pop hardware stores did when Home Depot and Lowe's emerged.

More Corporate, More Professionals

As more states and countries go legal, more talented people will enter the Cannabis industry. The level of competition is only going to get tougher. As more markets come online, there will be less stigma and fear around being in this space. This will attract professionals from more traditional industries to get involved. Also, as more institutional investors and established corporations enter the industry, it will force other participants to raise their standards of professionalism. And that's a good thing.

High Tech

There will be some kind of technology innovation that will completely disrupt the Cannabis industry as we know it. Perhaps it will be some discovery about the human endocannabinoid system. Or some sort of exponential leap in the ability to customize and optimize the variety and user pairing. I believe there will be some previously unimagined seismic shift in the next few years that will transform the industry completely.

There is a group of researchers who are working on mapping out the Cannabis genome. The vast majority of consumers and most medical professionals still have no idea how the various cannabinoids interact with the endocannabinoid system.

Hemp & Sustainability

Hemp has over 20,000 documented uses. Henry Ford built a hemp car that ran on hemp fuel. Hemp is a superfood and one of the best sources of plant-based nutrition. It absorbs carbon dioxide from the atmosphere. It absorbs toxins from the soil. It can be used to build energy-efficient houses, clothing, and much more.

Currently, research is being done to create hemp supercapacitors which can revolutionize anything that uses batteries. Hemp 3D printers, hemp fuel, and hemp polymers will disrupt the manufacturing, fossil fuel, and plastic industries, respectively.

Hemp ventures will become the new darling of impact investors as their community demands more environmentally responsible and regenerative opportunities to place capital into.

People Will Take Plant Medicines Seriously Again

Once more of the benefits of the Cannabis plant are discovered, embraced and utilized, people will explore other natural remedies. Ultimately, Cannabis legalization will facilitate a renewed appreciation for nature. Especially for the healing powers of plants. The emergence of Psilocybin for medical use and associated research is a direct result of the Cannabis movement and the drug policy activists who fueled it.

Although they may not be consciously aware of it, many

Cannabis consumers use the plant to self-medicate their mental health ailments. I look forward to a future in which health care professionals, especially mental health practitioners, are well versed in the healing properties of Cannabis. I imagine Cannabis facilitated therapy becoming a treatment that will offer many people relief from pain and suffering.

My hope is that the Cannabis movement helps the food is medicine movement and encourages people to learn more about food production and demand more natural, healthy, and regenerative agricultural practices. Better yet, grow your own food.

Cannabis Advertisement

Google, Facebook, and other major marketing mainstays still limit Cannabis content. This will change once Federal law changes. In my last book I asked, "How long until we're watching Cannabis Super Bowl commercials?" Shoutout to my friend Leighton Knowles, Founder of Wanderland Tea Shoppe: his CBD coffee product was part of in-stadium Super Bowl ads in early 2019. It will be interesting to see what happens when the big digital platforms stop discriminating against Cannabis businesses. It's only a matter of time until that happens. Until then, Cannabis entrepreneurs must be innovative and think outside the box.

Personally, I believe some of the most brilliant advertising ever has been in alcohol commercials. I look forward to seeing the world's leading advertising minds take on Cannabis brands. I eagerly await a wide range of Cannabis TV commercials, some that will likely make me roll my eyes with disgust and others that will make me feel proud of positive, healthy, and responsible Cannabis representation.

The End of Prohibition & Continued Opposition

Cannabis legalization has passed the tipping point. As long as industry leaders and Cannabis consumers engage in the political process, Federal Prohibition will end. This plant is the original social network and the business opportunity around it is the biggest thing for entrepreneurs since the birth of the Internet. Cannabis has been intertwined with human life for thousands of years and will no doubt be part of humanity's future.

History has demonstrated that time and time again, Cannabis has been used as a tool to push certain political agendas. Have no doubt about it, even after Cannabis prohibition ends, there will be groups and individuals who fundamentally oppose this industry and culture.

Some ways I can imagine this playing out is through class action lawsuits against licensed producers, demands for back taxes by the IRS, and fines from regulatory agencies like the FDA for activities that were not clearly regulated during the emergence of legal markets. I believe these sorts of strong-arming, extortionary tactics from powerful institutions are highly likely. Everybody wants to get a piece of the pot pie, whether they deserve a slice or not.

Over the course of humanity, no revolution has gone forward without a powerful reaction against it. Ethan Nadelmann told me, "I think we're going to continue to see people who don't want to let this battle go. There's also going to be people who are going to continue to discriminate against Cannabis but they can't through criminal prohibition, and so they're going to try to find other ways to do it. I think we still have a major battle ahead globally. Canada and parts of the U.S. are legalizing; still there are almost 200 countries to go. The international conventions need to be reformed, so there's a lot of work that needs to be done. The opposition is not just going to let go and we need to be careful because there are ways in which marijuana is promoted that could be problematic or create very bad media, and so we need to be attentive to that as well."

In order to protect the positive aspects of Cannabis culture, industry leaders will have to collaborate and support each other for the sake of the greater community.

Outstanding Questions

- What are we going to teach children about Cannabis?
- What will happen to other controlled substances (specifically plant-derived psychedelics) when Cannabis becomes legal?
- How will illegal drug cartels adjust to the legalization of Cannabis?
- What does Cannabis equity look like?
- How can we heal the victims and prisoners of the "War on Drugs?"
- What does getting the legal Cannabis industry right look like 50 years from now?

Part III:
A Higher Calling

"ONE HUMAN
—YOU—
CAN
MAKE A
SIGNIFICANT
IMPACT ON
THE CANNABIS INDUSTRY,
CANNABIS CULTURE,
AND ON
THE
WHOLE WORLD."

18.
Cannabis Justice For All

Cannabis has been a revolutionary and evolutionary force in humanity for thousands of years. Agriculture is the basis of modern civilization. And it's no coincidence that Cannabis is the most valuable crop in the world. The plant has played a major supporting role in the story of human civilization, helping humanity to blossom and flourish. Therefore, it is categorically unjust to punish or prevent the use of Cannabis, especially for therapeutic purposes.

Allow me to offer a brief history lesson.

Back in 6,000 BCE, before they were called "superfoods," hemp seeds and oils were used for nourishment in Ancient China.

By 4,000 BCE, hemp textiles were being used across Asia.

By 2,000 BCE, Cannabis was used medicinally in China and India. It was also used in sacred rituals in India.[68]

In more recent history, hemp rope and sails were used in ships by Vikings and Europeans, including on Columbus's voyages to the Americas. During World War II, the Marihuana Tax Act of 1937 was temporarily suspended so hemp could be grown to produce fiber for U.S. Navy ship ropes. Hemp played a pivotal role in

---

[68]It's extremely important for everyone in this industry to understand that in many cultures and traditions, Cannabis is considered sacred. Therefore, enthusiastically commercializing it can be viewed as profane and predatory.

helping humans navigate the waters of the world.

There are many more examples, and if you're interested, I highly recommend Michael Pollan's book, *Botany of Desire*, which chronicles the co-evolutionary relationship between Cannabis and humans.

For example, when the U.S. government ramped up its war on the plant in the 1960s, Cannabis growers adapted by moving indoors, implementing high tech methods that led to the breeding and proliferation of more potent Cannabis than what grew outdoors in the sun. When challenged by humans seeking to stifle it, Cannabis managed to evolve and grow stronger.

Pollan posits that the innate human desire for altering consciousness is part of the reason why we value Cannabis so much. Our willingness to pursue and defend that desire is part of the reason why Cannabis has been able to thrive and flourish on the biological evolutionary level.

America Was Built on Hemp

Cultivation of hemp was mandated by law in the Massachusetts, Virginia and Connecticut colonies. Beginning in 1631, hemp was legal tender for paying taxes in many of the American colonies and remained so for state taxes until the early 1800s.

Right now, we're living in the midst of a historical, civilization-defining, paradigm shift in which Cannabis policy can once again help to steer the course of human evolution. But to ensure we stay on the right path, we first need a revolution.

If you want to be active and successful in the Cannabis industry, you must first be willing to join this revolution.

Politics as Usual

Before there was a legal Cannabis industry, there was a counterculture political movement. The movement began around the time of the Vietnam War. It picked up serious momentum during the AIDS epidemic when LGBT activists and organizers realized the power of medical marijuana to relieve suffering in AIDS patients.[69] By the mid-1990's, the Cannabis movement started becoming what is now a legal and thriving industry.

What makes Cannabis a revolutionary industry is that it's rooted in activism and is fundamentally not all about the money. Although many non-Cannabis entrepreneurs, startups, and investors claim to be disruptive and innovative, the truth is many of them are unoriginal. In fact, they're trying to follow existing models through which they can generate predictable profit.

In Cannabis business, however, you're disruptive just by existing. How? Because most American and international institutions are still decidedly anti-Cannabis.

For example, in America, the criminal justice system, employment screening, public aid programs (e.g., food stamps, financial aid for education, public housing, etc.), child protective services, immigration policy, healthcare, media, and more are still explicitly anti-Cannabis. This negative attitude towards Cannabis is the direct result of a decades-long assault on minorities, the sick, the poor and anyone else who does not come from a life of

---

[69]RIP & Blessings to Dennis Peron for his activism

privilege.

PUNISHING PEOPLE FOR CANNABIS IS BAKED INTO MODERN AMERICAN LIFE ON THE INSTITUTIONAL LEVEL

If your Cannabis business helps to remedy those punitive precedents, you'll have a real chance at achieving revolutionary levels of success. The kind that changes the trajectories of thousands, millions, or even billions of Lives.

If you know there is an opportunity for your Cannabis business to make a positive impact on the world, why not aspire to that mission?

Remember, in Cannabis business, disruption is guaranteed.

As Kris Krane, long time advocate turned entrepreneur told me, "Industry is bringing more people into reform than ever before. Activism is growing exponentially. Industry is breeding activists. Industry has been and must be a gateway to reform." Let's make sure to continue that virtuous cycle.

The Revolutionary Nature of Cannabis Business

Trigger warning, I'm going to say some things you may find radical or that may even make you uncomfortable. Sometimes the truth hurts. You may not like what I say, and even disagree with me, and that's ok. Let's talk about the real issues, shall we?

THE PROHIBITION OF CANNABIS HAS BEEN A GATEWAY TO MANY INEXCUSABLE AND HARMFUL OUTCOMES IN OUR SOCIETY

Specifically, I'm referring to the modern American crises in public health, institutionalized racism, mass incarceration, and environmental destruction.

It's impossible to attribute a cost to the harms of Prohibition, but let's give it a try anyway. According to the Drug Policy Alliance, Federal and State governments have spent **over $1 trillion** of taxpayer money on the "War on Drugs." Unfortunately, these tax dollars haven't solved a damn thing—in fact, they've just created a new set of massive problems.

How do you quantify the value of a productive, healthy human life? What is that worth? I'd argue it's priceless.

Various U.S. government agencies (EPA, DOT, etc.) have used values ranging from $5 - $10 million dollars in models where the statistically derived value of a human life is factored into economic analysis.

Cannabis prohibition robbed millions of young people—mostly men of color—of the opportunity to actualize their potential. Let's assume the low-end statistical value of a human life to be $5 million. A 2010 Pew Charitable Trusts report[70] found that black men who experienced incarceration saw subsequent annual earnings reduced by 40%. Over the past few decades, that's a destruction of $2 million dollars of value for each of the 10 million black men arrested for nonviolent Cannabis-related offenses. That's at least $20 trillion of damages to men of color!

Not only did our public institutions rob these young people of

---

[70]The Pew Charitable Trusts, 2010. Collateral Costs: Incarceration's Effect on Economic Mobility. Washington, DC: The Pew Charitable Trusts.

the chance to grow and contribute, but in doing so they also destabilized their communities and inflicted multi-generational trauma that will be hurting our nation and the human collective for many years. Our politicians and so-called public servants justified these deliberately destructive schemes by demonizing Cannabis.

All Cannabis citizens (entrepreneurs, investors, employees, consumers, etc.), MUST know and internalize the information I'm going to share next, even if it seemingly has nothing to do with the financial statements of your Cannabis enterprise.

IN AMERICA, CANNABIS HAS BEEN EXPLOITED AS A TOOL FOR FURTHERING INSTITUTIONAL RACISM

Imagine if the legal Cannabis industry institutionalized investing into young men of color.

That seems sensible, fair, and doable to me.

And I think it'd be pretty revolutionary in the best possible way.

Perhaps I'm biased. The politics of my identity believe that Cannabis is to be used for elevating people's consciousness, capabilities, and quality of Life.

This history of Cannabis use for advancing racism is obvious and undeniable to anyone who has researched Prohibition.

In 1937, Cannabis was outlawed and written into our laws as "marihuana," a term created to associate Cannabis with Mexican migrants in the minds of white Americans.

In the 1930s and 40s, known as the *Reefer Madness* era, Cannabis was used to discriminate against black Jazz musicians.

In the 60s and 70s, Cannabis was associated with anti-war protesters and the hippie counterculture.

Since the start of the "War on Drugs" in the 1980s, Cannabis has been an excuse for discriminatory policing practices which have put millions of young men of color into prisons, where they're exploited as modern day slave laborers for the benefit of huge corporations and their shareholders.

One of Richard Nixon's top advisors admitted that the "War on Drugs" was created as a political tool to fight blacks and hippies.

> "We knew we couldn't make it illegal to be either against the war or black, but by getting the public to associate the hippies with marijuana and blacks with heroin and then criminalizing both heavily, we could disrupt those communities. We could arrest their leaders, raid their homes, break up their meetings, and vilify them night after night on the evening news. Did we know we were lying about the drugs? Of course we did."
>
> —John Ehrlichman
> Domestic Policy Chief, Nixon Administration[71]

If that doesn't infuriate you, then 1) you're probably racist and 2) you have no business being in the Cannabis business.

Do everyone a favor, and go earn your green elsewhere.

---

[71]https://www.cnn.com/2016/03/23/politics/john-ehrlichman-richard-nixon -drug-war-blacks-hippie/index.html

This intentional destruction of black and hispanic people's potential is nothing short of a crime against humanity. Perhaps in an alternate universe, Richard Nixon and Ronald Reagan are posthumously convicted of war crimes for all the lives they destroyed with the "War on Drugs." And then the casualties of the "War on Drugs" and their families would receive appropriate remuneration, restitution, and reparations.

The idealist in me believes it's possible, and the pragmatist is doubtful, especially as more greedy interests enter the industry with an ethos of profits over people, planet and purpose.

Infuriated by Injustice

You might be thinking, "Mike Z aren't you supposed to be Mr. Positivity? What happened to being the luckiest guy alive? You seem really serious all of a sudden."

The perpetuation of evil gets me angry. I believe you should be angry, too. Angry that so many people were robbed of opportunities to earn their livelihoods and exploited by systems designed to dehumanize them. Angry that government officials intentionally inflamed racial tensions and terrorized the citizens they are responsible for serving and protecting. Angry that millions of sick people have been deprived of medicine that they so desperately needed, while chemical corporations seek to maximize profits based on people's pain and suffering.

That's not the toxic kind of world I want to live in.

Anger is not necessarily a bad thing. It is a powerful emotion and that energy that can be used for good. Rather than being mad, I encourage you to do good. You may recall that my Cannabis activism was born out of anger. Anger at the injustice and suffering I had discovered. Let your anger fuel you to fight the good fight, to build a future in which justice triumphs, nature is respected, and humanity is bonded by an appreciation for all living beings. Don't let it blind you and turn you into a perpetrator who adds hate and suffering into the world.

A Sad United State of Affairs

I love America. I'm grateful beyond words that I was lucky enough to immigrate here and grow up in the U.S., a country where freedom and diversity are valued. To be an American is a great privilege that I've been blessed with.

But our country is not well. More Americans are sick than are healthy:

"About half of all American adults—117 million individuals—have one or more preventable chronic diseases, many of which are related to poor quality eating patterns and physical inactivity. These include cardiovascular disease, high blood pressure, type 2 diabetes, some cancers, and poor bone health. More than two-thirds of adults and nearly one-third of children and youth are overweight or obese. These high rates of overweightness, obesity, and chronic disease have persisted for more than two decades and come not only with increased health risks, but also high costs. In 2008, the medical costs associated with obesity were estimated to be $147 billion. In 2012, the total estimated cost of diagnosed diabetes was $245 billion, including $176 billion in direct medical costs and $69 billion in decreased productivity."[72]

We have a prescription-pill epidemic:

Data from the U.S. Centers for Disease Control and Prevention's National Center for Health Statistics and the U.S. census identified 351,630 opioid-related deaths from 1999 to 2016. In 2017 alone, there were over 49,000 opioid overdose deaths in America. That year, the Department of Health and Human Services declared the opioid addiction crisis to be a national public health emergency.

In addition to addiction problems, depression is on the rise in the United States. According to researchers at Columbia University's Mailman School of Public Health and the CUNY Graduate School of Public Health and Health Policy, depression rates increased significantly among Americans from 2005 to 2015.[73] Sadly, the World Health Organization called the U.S. the "most depressed" country in the world. In 2018, suicide was the #2 cause of death for Americans ages 10 – 34. If that's not indicative of a mental health crisis, I don't know what is.

We need healing and tons of it. I am not suggesting that Cannabis is a cure for all of Life's ills, but it has been used as a healing plant for thousands of years and I know it can help restore health in the United States and beyond.

[72]https://health.gov/dietaryguidelines/2015/guidelines/introduction/nutrition-and-health-are-closely-related/
http://www.cdc.gov/chronicdisease/overview/
[73]https://www.mailman.columbia.edu/public-health-now/news/depression-rise-us-especially-among-young-teens

As Real as it Gets

When used appropriately, Cannabis is a gateway towards greater mental health. I've met so many people around the country who have shared touching stories about how Cannabis got them off pills and saved their Lives. In fact, most Cannabis activists are born after the plant impacts their Lives, like when they experience the therapeutic benefits personally or witness a sick loved one who gets pain relief from the plant.

I'm going to share one of the wildest stories I've ever heard about Cannabis saving someone's Life.

I met a U.S. Army veteran who had seen combat on the front lines as a sniper. He had suffered several injuries in battle—both physical and psychological. The VA prescribed him a bunch of pills that turned him into a self-described zombie. Instead, he self-medicated his PTSD, chronic pain, and sleep issues with Cannabis. This man credits Cannabis with saving his Life. He's become a committed hemp advocate and environmentalist who works diligently to spread hemp education to fellow veterans and beyond.

Generally, I'd known him to be a super mellow, playful dude, who loves to joke and make people smile. A faithful vegan, he would enthusiastically share the benefits of a plant-based diet and warn anyone who would listen about the barbaric exploitation of animals by the modern food system. Beyond that, he'd encourage people to practice yoga and meditation to create more light and love in the world. I was shocked when he told me the story of how Cannabis saved his ex-wife's Life.

"I was going to kill my baby mama," he explained, looking me dead in the eyes. "After we separated, she got custody of my son and she wouldn't let me see him. I begged and I tried to reason with her, but she was a spiteful, psycho bitch," he continued.

"My son was the only thing in this world that I loved. And I was so fucking depressed, I just couldn't take it. I was committed; I decided to kill that bitch. I had it all planned out. I was going to break into her apartment, on her day off, when my son was at school, and I was going to shoot her in her stupid fucking face."

At this point, feeling the intensity and sincerity of his words, I was a little scared.

"So it was the big day: I had my gun, my knife, duct tape, gloves, I was ready to go. It was a beautiful day, warm sunshine, just beautiful. She lives uptown, in the Heights, so I went up there. And you know they got that good weed up in Wash Heights. So I picked up some haze and went to the park to smoke a joint. I'm puffing and I think to myself, 'Wow, what a beautiful day, the sun is shining, the birds are singing, I feel good, I don't want to leave this park.'

"So I roll some more, burn it, and think 'Now this is going to be a lot of work and the cops might catch me and they might kill me. And if I kill her, my son will be sad, cause that bitch is his mom. Then he'll be mad at me, and if I'm in jail or dead, who will take care of him?'

"So I smoked some more haze, it was some good shit yo. Then I think, 'Fuck this bitch, she ain't worth it. I'm not going to let her ruin my Life. I'll go to court and tell the judge that this stupid puta ain't letting me see my son and a boy needs to have a dad. I'm an Army veteran, I pay my child support, the judge will tell her she can't do this shit to me.'

"And that's what I did. Now I see my son and it's all good, even though I hated his mom, I learned to forgive her. So thank God for weed, because if I didn't get high that day, I would've killed her. Cannabis saved my ex-wife's Life."

He laughed a big, hearty laugh. I had no idea what to make of it, other than Cannabis saves lives. The plant promotes homeostasis. Cannabis can help neutralize even the most intense anger or depression. It can bring people back from emotional extremes.

On the surface, Cannabis saved the day and this story had a happy ending. Digging deeper, however, reveals a tragic tale.

Cannabis Prohibition Kills Veterans

In the last 10 years, more veterans have died of suicide than the number of U.S. troops killed during the Vietnam War. On average 22 veterans commit suicide every day. According to several veterans-turned-Cannabis-activists I've spoken to, that official statistic underreports the truth.

A National Institute of Health study found that over 60% of veterans suffer from chronic pain and approximately 20% suffer from PTSD. According to an American Legion (the nation's largest wartime veterans' service organization) survey of veteran households, 82% of respondents wanted to have Cannabis available as a federally-legal treatment. 92% were in favor of greater medical research.

Yet, due to the federal classification of Cannabis as a schedule 1 drug with no medical value, the Veteran's Affairs (VA) medical system cannot recommend or help pay for Cannabis medicine, even in states where medical Cannabis is legal. Dangerous opioids and antidepressants—no problem. Except there's a huge problem, the opioid epidemic.

Until recently, VA doctors weren't even allowed to talk to their patients about medical Cannabis. The VA's official policy states that: "Veteran participation in state marijuana programs does not affect eligibility for VA care and services." However, some veterans have discovered otherwise, losing VA home loan eligibility, employment, and firearm permits for disclosing use of medical Cannabis. All over America, veterans are turning to medical Cannabis for relief. Unfortunately, they have to pay for it out of pocket, and often are in the position of having to decide between their health and their financial security. This is no way to treat the people who risked their lives for our nation.

No wonder some of the most effective Cannabis activists I know are veterans.

The Revolution Will Not be Vaporized

The Cannabis plant, the Cannabis movement, and the Cannabis business together make a triumvirate that can triumph in transforming humanity in positive ways. Due to the intersectional nature of Cannabis, the disruption that will result from Cannabis innovation will be institutional and revolutionary.

As I see it, the Cannabis revolution is a fight to elevate the collective human consciousness and to create a more healthy, compassionate, just, free, and sustainable world.

It's already happening.

Thanks to Cannabis business, hundreds of thousands of people are getting or have already had their past marijuana-related offenses expunged, removing from them the scarlet letter of criminal that carries with it significant collateral consequences.

Committed Cannabis advocates have paved the way for research on MDMA and psilocybin assisted therapy as an alternative way to help heal people suffering from PTSD, depression, addiction, and other health issues.

Young people are developing an interest in farming and permaculture because of hemp.

These small steps will ripple out into significant positive impact for the next generation and beyond.

That being said, I believe the entire Cannabis community needs to unite and demand even more when it comes to Cannabis justice. For example, to expunge criminal records is not enough. That's the bare minimum. The people who have been victims of the war on drugs are living with the trauma of being institutionalized. They need healing and rehabilitation. Wouldn't it be just for that support to be funded by law enforcement budgets?

Leadership Matters

To be clear, I don't view Cannabis as a panacea. To create solutions for America's public health crises, institutional racism, and broken criminal justice system will require revolutionary leadership, unselfish teamwork, and radical innovation.

THE SUCCESS OR FAILURE OF THE GLOBAL CANNABIS EMPOWERMENT MOVEMENT WILL DEPEND ON THE QUALITY OF LEADERSHIP THAT WORKS TO STEER THE HISTORICALLY POWERFUL FORCE THAT IS CANNABIS.

Fortunately, this industry is full of brilliant leaders who are highly conscious about the issues I've talked about in this chapter and who are motivated to help solve them.[74] The wealth creation of Cannabis business success will empower mission-driven leaders to tackle these bigger issues.

After all, those who approach Cannabis business with the high mindset see it as a mechanism through which it's possible to create new regenerative, inclusive, and compassionate institutions that promote justice and encourage all plants and humans to flower into their greatest potential together.

What part of the solution do you want to be responsible for?

How will you show up?

Are you going to be that revolutionary Cannabis leader who changes the world?

---

[74]And the many issues I didn't cover, including the problems of modern agriculture, inequitable and unsafe food systems, and natural resource scarcity.

"Think about the impact that our work will have on culture and society. To truly succeed, we have to work together with regulators, consumers and each other to help shape a healthy industry, which benefits the public. We've seen immense failures in many industries that Cannabis gets compared to. Some examples would be events like the opioid crisis, the most recent vaping scandal, and the long history of negative health impacts of smoking and drinking alcohol. The Cannabis industry can choose a different path, or even help curb the negative impacts of those other products. Since the Cannabis industry is so new, much of what happens will be driven by entrepreneurs like us, and we have this amazing opportunity and also the responsibility to create an industry that benefits everyone."

—Kevin Chen,
CEO and Co-Founder, Hyasynth Bio

19.

Cannabis Leadership Principles

> "Leadership isn't to give a good speech, it isn't to boss people around, or to stay organized. It's to empower and encourage others to create their own path."
>
> —Kayvan Khalatbari,
> Founding Partner, Denver Relief, Denver Relief Consulting,
> Board of Directors, Minority Cannabis Business Association

> "Leading with humility is the thing I have most success with. I'm a firm believer in servant leadership. Serving the needs of my community and my employees before profit."
>
> —Christie Lunsford,
> CEO, The Hemp Biz Conference

> "The most important decision any leader makes are the decisions that relate to the people he or she is serving. How I take care of the people working with me. On the smallest micro level, that's what's most important: that everybody who works with me and around me feels well taken care of, well rewarded, and happy doing what they're doing."
>
> —Steve DeAngelo,
> Co-Founder, Harborside Dispensary Group
> Author of *The Cannabis Manifesto*

It's difficult to define leadership and even more challenging to define great leadership. It's kind of like pornography—you know it when you see it. I will offer that an indisputable, defining element of leadership is the willingness to take greater responsibility for outcomes.

Leadership begins on a personal level. First and foremost, you must take responsibility for yourself and the impact of your actions, intended and unintended. Often, taking responsibility requires sacrifice. Sacrificing what is comfortable or easy for what is right. Sacrificing what you want for what benefits the greater good. To do this consistently and to hold others to that same high standard is the hallmark of great leadership.

> "The most important decisions that I make as a leader are deciding how to show up, and to show up as my best self, ready for anything. As somebody willing to put himself in that position, it means people are going to look towards you for answers, for help, for guidance, for motivation. As an entrepreneur, as a leader, you have to be willing to put yourself in a position to field these kinds of questions over your own personal interest, at any given time."
>
> —Mike Garganese,
> Co-Founder, Lola Lola, Hilani, & Pluto

Sounds glamorous doesn't it?

Leadership begins with knowing your values and having an authentic desire to be in service and care of others. To lead implies being responsible for not only yourself but for all those who follow your lead.

Great leaders are developed and they learn from other great leaders. This industry only exists because, for decades, brave people took the huge risks necessary to keep it moving. If you intend to be a leader or even a participant in this industry, you damn well better honor those who risked everything to blaze the trail that we now walk. Make it one of your Cannabis leadership principles to honor the elders, patriots, and pioneers of the Cannabis movement.

> "If we're truly giving credit to and appreciating the folks [before] us that have done everything that they have to get this industry to where it's at today, we have to continue being uncomfortable and making others uncomfortable with progress and with what's right. That's the only way we're going to fully realize an industry that is for everybody. That is different from everything else we have out there that is creating so many issues in this world right now—capitalism at all costs. The Cannabis industry has a huge opportunity to be something different, and I hope people really absorb what that means. [That may] mean making tough decisions and, maybe, not even winning out individually at the end of the day, but knowing that it's best for the common good and broader [purpose] of what we're trying to do here."
>
> —Kayvan Khalatbari,
> Founding Partner, Denver Relief, Denver Relief Consulting,
> Board of Directors, Minority Cannabis Business Association

> "I've been putting out a call that we not just create a new industry with Cannabis. Instead, we must create a new *kind* of industry with Cannabis. That means taking the lessons that this plant teaches us—respect for nature, gentleness, compassion, and generosity—and building them into our business models."

—Steve DeAngelo,
Co-Founder, Harborside Dispensary Group,
Author of *The Cannabis Manifesto*

How can we best honor the pioneers and do what's best for the common good? I'll let someone more qualified answer that question: Ethan Nadelmann.

Ethan, the founder of the Drug Policy Alliance, is one of Cannabis freedom's greatest pioneers. He opened and led the public debate on Cannabis in the 80s and 90s and put together the campaigns and financing for the first 7 medical marijuana legalization initiatives in the late 90s, and many more Cannabis legalization campaigns, until his retirement in 2017. His 2014 TED talk on "Why We Need to End the War on Drugs" has almost 2 million views. And if you haven't seen it yet, you should get on that. When he spoke at one of my High NY events, Ethan told an audience full of eager, aspiring Cannabis entrepreneurs, investors, and advocates that because of all the work he's done to make a legal Cannabis industry possible, "I'm your daddy." It was epic. But I digress.

> "My hope, of course, is that people who have gotten involved in this industry and people who are getting involved will understand that there is a special obligation, some sort of consciousness which should be part of what they do because of how this industry emerged. This industry emerged on the backs of tens of millions of people, oftentimes poor people of color—but not just people of color—getting victimized because of the war on marijuana. It came about because wealthy philanthropists from across the political spectrum were

willing to put money into this, not because of economic or financial opportunity, but because it was the right thing to do. It came about because of activists like me, and a whole bunch of others, who cared about this for those sorts of reasons. In reality, I think that 95% of the people getting involved don't give a damn, and they're not going to give a damn. I think that understanding the origins of your opportunity and giving back in some way, whether it's becoming a financial donor to drug policy reform, whether it's by the way you run your company, will yield dividends in ways that can't necessarily be calculated in dollars and cents up front."

—Ethan Nadelmann,
Founder, Drug Policy Alliance

Stay true to the Cannabis leadership principles discussed in this chapter. Internalize them, practice them, teach them, refer to them in times of doubt, embody them.

Now that you've read this book, you have no excuse not to do the right thing. Take responsibility. Be a leader.

20.

The Power of One

> "Never doubt that a small group of thoughtful, committed citizens can change the world; indeed, it's the only thing that ever has."
>
> —Margaret Mead, Anthropologist

What do you, Cannabis, and Cannabis businesses have in common? All have the power to be transformative agents of change. Especially when combined together in a good way.

Even though I've said it already, I will remind you that we're living in the midst of a paradigm shift in which Cannabis policy can dramatically alter the course of human civilization.

Hemp and Cannabis, if utilized and integrated into society in a responsible, conscious, and generative way, can facilitate healing for the whole planet.

Will you be one of those history-making leaders that leaves a legacy of creating a brighter future for all to enjoy?

That may sound dramatic or ridiculous to you, and if so, I understand how you feel. You might consider yourself to be just another average Joe or Jill who wants to work in the Cannabis business or has a dream of being a Cannabis entrepreneur. Or perhaps you're a seasoned business person who has enough painful life experience to think that being idealistic just isn't realistic. That's ok, too.

If you'd have told me 6 years ago that I'd write 2 books about Cannabis, educate hundreds of thousands of people about the plant, build one of the world's largest Cannabis community groups, and live my dream of being a successful Cannabis entrepreneur and business coach, I'd have told you, "Get real!"

If you'd have told me that I'd collaborate with Cannabis industry OGs or that I'd consult with universities, governments, and corporations on how to enter the legal Cannabis industry, I'd have said, "Cool story, bro."

And if you'd have told me that I'd train aspiring Cannabis entrepreneurs on behalf of the U.S. Government-sponsored National Science Foundation, I'd have told you, "You're absolutely crazy."

For better or for worse, nobody ever told me any of the above. I didn't know what was possible for me in the Cannabis business. I definitely didn't know that I was capable of all of the above. I just loved the plant and knew that I wanted to make a difference in this world. Deep inside, I felt like Cannabis would be my gateway to something bigger, something greater, beyond myself. Because it always had been.

In case nobody has ever told you what's possible for you with the Cannabis plant or in the Cannabis industry, allow me to tell you that the possibilities are beyond what your imagination is capable of conceiving. Take your wildest Cannabis business success dream, bring it to mind, see it, savor it, take a few deep breaths as if you have made it real, and then understand that what's possible for you is something even greater, something that you can't even fathom yet. If only there was a consciousness-expanding plant that could help you think differently about your own self-imposed limitations…

Remember Nial DeMena, the Green American Dream? He told me several times that his business has gone farther than he'd ever imagined.

I'm not saying that it will come easily or that it's a sure thing—no, far from it. Blood, sweat, tears, and time are all necessary to make anything significant happen. Just know that it's possible.

ONE HUMAN CAN MAKE A SIGNIFICANT IMPACT ON THIS INDUSTRY, ON THIS MOVEMENT, AND ON THIS PLANET

Let my story and the stories of the leaders in this book serve as proof. No doubt they've all experienced and shared the absolutely transformative power of Cannabis many times over.

Now that I have shared the truth, I invite you to step into your power, own it, and use it for good. There are people counting on you. The community is counting on you. And the Cannabis plant is counting on you to do the right thing and be a force for positive change.

In case you don't believe me, maybe you'll believe Shanel Lindsay, who was recently re-appointed to the Massachusetts Cannabis Advisory Board, where she is helping to craft regulations for Massachusetts's adult-use Cannabis market, and no doubt having a massive impact in the industry and broader Cannabis community.

"One thing that has amazed me more than anything when I look back over these last five years now is how I never would have believed how powerful my own voice could become. I think people underestimate how much power they have... a lot of people that are [reading] this are in places where Cannabis hasn't been fully implemented or legalized yet. Frankly, that's almost everywhere, and what you must realize is that your voice—in your neighborhood, in your community, at your local municipal meetings—[has so] much power to move the needle when it comes to the way that people think about Cannabis. Just by being who you are, just by sharing your story...you can make a change in the world. You can make a business, you can do what you love, you can do all of those things in one. That can be the case for so many more Cannabis entrepreneurs."

—Shanel Lindsay,
Founder & President, Ardent Cannabis
Member of the Massachusetts Cannabis Advisory Board

Shanel knows what's possible for you. I know what's possible for you. And I suspect that every leader featured in this book knows what's possible for you. So, are you ready to use your voice, to own your power, and to be that world-changing leader?

The time is now.

"You're the one thing between you and the next level."

—Asher Troppe,
CEO & Co-Founder, Tress Capital

21.
Your Highest Self

"You will find true success and happiness if you have only one goal—there really is only one—and that is this: to fulfill the highest most truthful expression of yourself as a human being. You want to max out your humanity by using your energy to lift yourself up, your family and the people around you."

—Oprah Winfrey, Media Mogul

By now, you've observed that the successful Cannabis business leaders highlighted in this book have a lot in common. This is especially true when it comes to mindset and habits. That's no coincidence. I want to emphasize one characteristic of all highly effective humans. Something that is true beyond Cannabis and beyond business.

Here it is: they all consume Cannabis. Just kidding.

From J.P. Morgan, to Google, to Cannabis business, and everywhere in between, one common characteristic of all high achievers is a growth mindset. Especially when it comes to themselves. Regardless of the millions of dollars of wealth created or the millions of lives they've impacted, high achievers never stop working on personal growth and development.

Several of the people featured in this book could be retired and hanging out on the beach, puffing on tropical landraces, enjoying the high Life.

Instead, they're pushing themselves, grinding, working to make the most of the gifts and opportunities they've been blessed with. These people are working on themselves and on their businesses in an effort to leave things better than they found them.

> "Your only competition in Life is yourself and your job is to put you out of business. What I mean by that is take all that you do today, teach somebody how to do it more efficiently than you do, and put bigger [stuff] on your plate."
>
> —Garyn Angel
> CEO, Magical Butter

Guess what? If you want to be like the Cannabis business leaders featured in this book, you have to share this commitment to personal development. Cultivate yourself into the most potent, excellent, highest version of yourself possible. Doing so is one of the greatest gifts you can offer to the people you love and your community.

Higher and Higher

Many spiritual leaders have said that humans have a moral obligation to become the best version of themselves possible and to constantly refine their character. Why? Because this concept of self-actualization is the ultimate act of appreciation and respect for Life. Scientists argue that the drive to thrive and expand is the one natural evolutionary instinct shared by all forms of Life.

Here are some ways the Cannabis industry's top leaders work on developing their skills:

> "Continue to challenge yourself and put yourself outside

your comfort zone. When you feel like you're hanging from the edge of a cliff by literally a finger, you can take solace in the fact that you're growing internally."

—Holly Alberti,
Founder, Healthy Headie Lifestyle
Director of Marketing, iAnthus

"Seek out people, organizations, and activities, centered around opening you up and shifting the way you look at and perceive things to help give yourself an edge. Open yourself up more. Some of the things that I've done to help with this have been personal development coaching from people like Mike Z and with organizations like Landmark."

—Mike Garganese,
Co-Founder, Lola Lola, Hilani, & Pluto

"Constantly moving into new roles and taking on new responsibilities."

—Amanda Reiman, PhD
Director of Community Relations, Flow Kana

"I actually just got my first career coach. I think that's a really important thing [for me] to be able to take a litmus test on [my] own leadership skills, to be able to strip down conversations or interactions with someone, dissect them and find new ways that I can approach an issue...The better I am able to understand my own emotions in a situation, organize them, and communicate well with my team, the more it helps everybody. So, as leaders, we never stop working on ourselves and you should never stop trying to relate to the people that work for you."

—Caroline Phillips,
Founder, National Cannabis Festival

> "We have a monthly team leadership offsite to work on planning, on ourselves, and on caring for our employees. We listen. We ask our employees and clients for feedback constantly. We try to create a rich feedback culture, so people feel comfortable being honest, expressing, and being heard."

—Peter Barsoom,
CEO, Nuka Enterprises

Becoming your highest self is a process that requires getting help from multiple teachers. When I entered Cannabis, I had no idea what I was doing. But I knew how to connect with people. So I reached out to and interviewed the industry's top leaders across business, policy, medicine, activism, culture, and more. I leveraged the expertise of people who had more knowledge and experience than I did. That's what you must do if you want to succeed.

> "We have a team of advisers that come from very, very different industries and they're not shy about speaking up, which is exactly what we want."

—Giadha Aguirre De Carcer,
Founder & CEO, New Frontier Data

Mentors and Coaches are Essential

Mentors will accelerate your learning curve, expand your network, and help you uncover and avoid blind spots. Plus, in this industry, they might share with you the dankest buds you've ever tasted. Mentors must be people whom you admire and want to be like. They are the people who are either living your dream life or who have already lived it. They are the models of success for you to follow.

> "Work with someone who's done it before. Entrepreneurs are incredible, someone that we all look up to and we all want to be. We all want to act on our dreams and visions and so I like to think of entrepreneurs as heroes. When you think about heroes, you realize in history, and even today, every hero has a mentor."
>
> —Francis Priznar,
> SVP and Chief Mentor, The Arcview Group

Bill Gates, Eric Schmidt and many other prolific business leaders agree that, "Everyone can benefit from coaching." Many executives, high achieving professionals, and all elite athletes invest in coaching. According to a study of senior executives at Fortune 1000 companies who received coaching, the average return was 5.7 times the investment.[75] Not only will you grow as a result of working with a coach, but you will also learn coaching skills which can be applied to developing your teammates and employees.

Coaching is not for low or poor performers—quite the contrary, it's most often utilized by high performers, those who hold themselves to higher standards for success and thus want to execute at their maximum potential.[76] The people who get the

---

[75]McGovern, J., Lindemann, M., Et Al. (2001). Maximizing the Impact of Executive Coaching: Behavioral Change, Organizational Outcomes, and Return on Investment. The Manchester Review, 6(1).

[76]Oprah, Princess Diana, Nelson Mandela, Leonardo DiCaprio, Serena Williams, Steve Jobs, Jeff Bezos have all hired Life & Business coaches.

best results out of coaching are those who aren't afraid of the commitment and hard work necessary to evolve. And they have the humility to know that they can grow and get even better.

If you don't have at least one solid, consistent mentor or coach supporting you in your journey of becoming your highest self, then make it your priority to find one as soon as you finish reading this book. Find someone who has achieved mastery. Find someone who sees more potential and ability in you than you see in yourself. Find someone who inspires you to want to become your highest self. If you can find all of those qualities in one person, fantastic! If not, get a few coaches, mentors, or teachers with different specialties.

> Who is wise? He who learns from every person.
>
> —Jewish proverb

Honor your coaches, mentors, teachers, and whoever supports you in your growth (friends and family) by regularly expressing your gratitude for them.[77] Don't wait until it's too late. Do it now. Demonstrate respect by applying the lessons they teach you.

Once you feel sufficiently competent and qualified to do so, pay it forward by becoming a mentor and helping others in their growth journeys.

---

[77]If you enjoyed this book, some excellent ways to express your gratitude are by leaving me a 5 star review on Amazon.com and/or by recommending the book to someone you know.

22.
Above and Beyond

By reading this book, your journey into the Cannabis industry has already begun. Here is a reminder of everything you have now learned:

* why Cannabis business is revolutionary by nature
* whether or not the Cannabis business is right for you
* what it takes to succeed in weed
* why Cannabis activism is mandatory
* how to build relationships with industry insiders
* how to attract high quality Cannabis investors
* the principles of Cannabis leadership
* that one individual can change the entire industry and the entire world

Beyond that, hopefully you've been convinced that anything is possible for you through Cannabis business. Not just serious income, but also positive outcomes.

In case you weren't convinced, I've saved one of the most potent, mind-blowing truths for last: you have a better chance of succeeding in Cannabis business than every single person I interviewed.

That's because none of today's industry leaders had *The Cannabis Business Book* to guide them. None of us had the unwritten rules, the Cannabis leadership principles, the traps, the tips, or the insights from seasoned professionals when we started our

Cannabis business journeys. Yet, we've all achieved success. You now have an advantage that none of us had. Let that inspire confidence in you.

It took me 6 years to acquire and synthesize this knowledge. It took reading dozens of books, attending hundreds of events, investing thousands of dollars, taking risks, and making countless mistakes to give you this book.

Now that you have this knowledge, it's time for you to do the work. Do it well. Do it consistently. Do it with integrity. Most importantly, do it in the service of a higher purpose than financial gain.

Apply the high mindset to all you do and strive to be like Cannabis—indiscriminately generous, uplifting, and restorative. Prioritize outcomes over income.

Become rooted in that mindset and you will be on your way to making money every day, doing what you love, and making this world a better place.

We Can Get Higher Together

I began this book by inviting you to get high with me. I'm going to end the same way.

If this book was the beginning of your Cannabis business journey, you've likely learned that the industry is much more complicated than simply getting high and printing money. Perhaps you're overwhelmed by the possibilities, not sure what to do next, where to start, or how to integrate this book's teachings into practice.

If you're already in the industry and committed to Cannabis business, I hope this book inspired you, affirmed your efforts, and reminded you of the power and responsibility you have in shaping this industry and in creating a healthier, more just future.

Whatever the case may be, I want to hear from you so we can get higher together.

I invite you to contact me at www.MichaelZaytsev.com/contact if you want my help with:

- Cannabis Business Development (the other CBD)
- Cannabis Communications, PR, & Media strategy
- Fundraising and Investor Relations
- Life Coaching or Business Coaching
- Connections to anyone in this book (and beyond)
- Event Production and Marketing
- Building Community
- Feedback on your Cannabis business plan
- Booking me to speak at your event
- Personal and professional development
- Product testing and reviews
- Finding a mentor
- anything else you can think of

Keep the High Times Rolling

What kind of coach would I be if I didn't give you homework?

#1 Write down your biggest takeaways from this book. Otherwise you'll forget. Write yourself a one page book report to guarantee that the lessons stick. Do this today.

#2 If you don't have a mentor or coach, find one ASAP. Begin by mapping out what characteristics that person must have. Think about where to find people like that. Who do you know that can connect you with that type of person? Ask for an intro. If you already have mentors or coaches, write one of them a one page letter of gratitude for what they've given you. Do this today.

#3 Determine what the next investment in your Cannabis education will be. Maybe it's reading another Cannabis book, taking a class, or even growing a plant. Whatever you choose, create a SMART goal around, and start working on it within 7 days.

#4 Determine your strengths and weaknesses. What are you really good at? What are your top skills? What are your flat spots? There are several professional assessments you can take for this.[78] And you can email 5 people who know you really well and ask them to give you honest feedback by answering these questions: (do this within 7 days)

> 1. What are my strengths? What can you count on me for? (Please state 2-3 things)

> 2. What are my weaknesses? What can you not count on me for? (Please state 2-3 things)

> 3. What is my superpower? What am I the best at in the

---

[78]Gallup's Strengthsfinder and UPenn's Character Strengths Survey are two that I like.

world?

#5 **Invest in your Cannabis network.** Go on Meetup or Eventbrite and find a local Cannabis networking opportunity. Or find a local NORML or Women Grow chapter. Attend a Cannabis event. Meet the people in the community. Connect with them, learn from them, offer value, and build relationships. Do this within 30 days.

#6 **Listen to the Cannabis business insider interviews.** This will reinforce the teachings and also provide you with much more information about the industry and what it takes to succeed. Get access now at www.MichaelZaytsev.com/bookbonus (listen to 1 - 3 interviews per week for the next 90 days)

#7 **Listen to "The Cannabis Business Coach Podcast" where I interview and coach the highest achievers in Cannabis Business.** Available on Apple and Spotify and with video on my website. Do this every week on Thursdays when new episodes are released.

#8 **Celebrate.** Honor the work you're doing, reflect on your progress regularly, and treat yourself in some way after you finish each assignment. Maybe even treat yourself to some Cannabis.

23.
All Praise to The Most High

"Sometimes when you're in a dark place you think you've been buried, but you've actually been planted. Bloom."

—Christine Caine,
Author & Activist

Six years after my surgery, my arm still hurts. The scar tissue around my repaired nerve, the lack of sensitivity down my right forearm, and the distorted sensation in my pinky and ring finger are still with me every day. I thought I'd get used to it by now and that it'd eventually begin feeling normal. It hasn't.

When it rains, my arm knows. When it gets cold, my arm gets stiff. And in the rare case when I don't do yoga for two consecutive days, my arm reminds me with a dose of pain that I'm not taking care of business.

After recovering from surgery, I had to re-learn how to use my right arm and hand. In doing so, I inadvertently learned some bad habits, like compensating for the limited range of motion in my elbow with too much movement from my shoulder. After four long years of physical therapy, my elbow recovered to a level that several doctors told me would be impossible. How? Because I was (and still am) ruthlessly committed to my rehabilitation and physical therapy, no matter how painful it is. For the last two years, I've been working on fixing the shoulder issues I've developed which have offered me a whole new flavor of chronic pain.

And for that pain, I'm grateful.

It reminds me how lucky I am to be alive.

My physical pain—all of that shit—is the fertilizer from which my mental fortitude grows. And I need all the mental fortitude I can get; after all, I'm in the Cannabis business. There's still plenty of work to do.

When I was bedridden for several months at age 24, I had a lot of time to ponder. Why did this "freak" accident happen to me? What had I done to deserve all this pain? I feared that I'd never have a normal, healthy Life again. I felt buried. Buried in fear, shame, and hopelessness.

How come I didn't die? Why was I even alive?

I didn't know the answers until that fateful Cannabis meetup when I learned the deeper truths about my favorite plant and made a decision about my place in this world.

When I felt buried, I didn't know yet that I was a seed. Planted with a chance to grow and bloom into something strong and beautiful. I didn't know that I would help breathe Life into the Cannabis community and join a rich ecosystem of inspired people doing the same.

What if I had died that day? What if I die today or tomorrow? That would suck. There's so much more that I want to experience and contribute in this world. But I can only be responsible for doing my best while I am here, now.

Reflecting on the time and space that my Life has occupied, I feel like the luckiest man alive. It has nothing to do with the dollars I've made and spent. It's not because of the achievements I've accomplished, nor the recognitions I've received. It's all because of the people I've met on my journey. The connections, experiences, and relationships I've received—largely thanks to Cannabis—are the greatest gifts I could have ever asked for. They are the air, sunlight, water, and soil from which I rise.

And so I close in gratitude, giving thanks to all of those people for nourishing my spirit. I especially thank the pioneers and leaders of the Cannabis movement who created the possibility for me to have this opportunity. Thank you to the readers for buying this book and entering a mutually beneficial relationship with me. I hope it will extend beyond these pages.

Thank you to my ancestors, my grandparents, my parents, and my dear friends and loved ones for nurturing my growth and for cultivating me.

Thank you Cannabis, for without you this book wouldn't exist and I might still be buried.

Above all, I thank the Most High. Whether you call it God, the Universe, Mother Nature, the Great Mystery, or by any other name, I invite you to give thanks.

Thank you for Cannabis.

Thank you for the people and relationships I've been gifted.

Thank you for this beautiful Life.

Acknowledgments

Thank you to every single person who I interviewed for this book:

Alain Bankier, Amanda Reiman, Amber Senter, Andrew Defries, Asher Troppe, Ben Pollara, Brian Vicente, Caroline Phillips, Casey O'Neil, Chloe Villano, Christian Hageseth, Christie Lundsford, Cy Scott, Danielle Schumacher, Danny Danko, Dave Tran, David Hess, David Hua, Eileen Konieczny, Emily Paxhia, Ethan Nadelmann, Evan Nison, Francis Priznar, Garyn Angel, Giadha Aguirre de Carcer, Holly Alberti-Evans, Jack Cole, Jake Plowden, Jim McAlpine, Jon Braveman, Kayvan Khalatbari, Kevin Chen, Kris Krane, Laura Lagano, Leo Bridgewater, Mara Gordon, Mark Doherty, Mike Garganese, Mowgli Holmes, Nelson Guerrero, Nial DeMena, Peter Barsoom, Rhory Gould, Sal Barnes, Scott Greiper, Shanel Lindsay, Steve DeAngelo, Steven Phan.

Thank you to my official editor, who is also the person I've shared more Cannabis with than any other human, Alex "Sasha Grafit" Grabovskiy.

Thank you to my unofficial editor and long-time High NY champion, Dmitriy Ioselevich of 17 Communications.

Thank you Jake Wyrick for being so generous with your time and friendship.

Thank you to Angela Mou, Mona Zhang, Ramon Torres, Saif Khan my High NY OG's for helping in the early days.

Thank you Todd Hinden for always showing up and for your commitment to Cannabis. Thanks for believing in me and for always being willing to lend a helping hand, often with a doobie in it.

Thank you Socrates S. Smith for your chit chat, checklists, challenges, comedy, and for your activism. An OG's OG.

Thank you Toto. The book is done! For real this time.

Thank you to the whole High NY community and every person who has ever supported a High NY event in any way.

Thank you to my friends and family who keep me grounded and inspired. You know who you are. You mean the world to me.

Thank you to all my coaching clients for trusting me and for allowing me to serve you with the best of my abilities.

Thank you to the ManKind Project, the National Science Foundation, the New Leaders Council, Google, J.P. Morgan, Claremont McKenna College, Stuyvesant, the US of A, and all the great institutions I've had the privilege to be a part of.

Thank you to all the great mentors and teachers who have schooled me.

Thank you to anyone who has shared their platform and given me the chance to spread the good word about the good herb.

Thank you to anyone who has ever shared Cannabis and/or Cannabis education with me.

Thank you to everyone who purchased my book.

Thank you Rasta.

Thank you Cannabis and Mother Earth for providing.

I acknowledge that I'm privileged to be able to write this book and do this work. I want to acknowledge those who are less fortunate, especially all who have suffered due to the War on Drugs and Cannabis prohibition. This book is for you.

About The Author

Michael Zaytsev, or Mike Z, is the best-selling author known as The Cannabis Business Coach™.

Mike Z began his career working at J.P. Morgan and then Google. After facilitating an internal Leadership and Teamwork training program at Google, Mike Z became obsessed with high performance coaching. In 2014, he received Coaching Certification and started his coaching business.

Mike Z has engaged audiences all over the world on a full spectrum of Cannabis topics. His 2016 TEDx Talk invited the mainstream to start "Thinking Differently About Cannabis."

As the award-winning Founder and CEO of High NY, one of the world's largest Cannabis Meetup communities, Mike Z has personally produced Cannabis education events and networking opportunities for thousands of people. He's raised thousands of dollars for Cannabis justice nonprofits. Mike Z has co-created more than a million organic and original Cannabis-positive media impressions to challenge the anti-Cannabis stigma.

In 2019, Mike Z served as a Cannabis Industry Mentor for the National Science Foundation's Innovation Corps entrepreneurship training program, working with a grant winning team from Drexel University's Nyheim Plasma Institute.

Michael is a proud alumnus of Stuyvesant High School and Claremont McKenna College.

The Cannabis Business Coach Podcast

The Cannabis Business Coach™ interviews and coaches the highest performing entrepreneurs and investors in Cannabis.

Available on Apple Podcasts, Spotify, YouTube, and at www.MichaelZaytsev.com.

@HiMikeZ

Made in the USA
Middletown, DE
26 April 2021

38492173R00124